Happy Housewives

ReganBooks
An Imprint of HarperCollins*Publishers*

Happy Housewives

Darla Shine

HarperCollins books may be purchased for educational, business, or sales promotional use. For information please write: Special Markets Department, HarperCollins Publishers Inc., 10 East 53rd Street, New York, NY 10022.

FIRST EDITION

Designed by Paula Russell Szafranski

Printed on acid-free paper

Library of Congress Cataloging-in-Publication Data has been applied for.

ISBN 0-06-0859202-2

05 06 07 08 09 WBC/RRD 10 9 8 7 6 5 4 3 2 1

I dedicate this book to all

the mamas out there.

STEP 1
STEP 2

STEP 3
STEP 4
STEP 5
STEP 6
STEP 7
STEP 8
STEP 9
STEP 10

CONTENTS

Introduction   1

Please Stop Whining!   5

Be Proud! Being an At-Home Mom Is
the Most Important Job   17

Stop Looking Like a Housewife   31

Make Your Marriage a Priority   53

Bond with Your Home   69

Get Back in the Kitchen   97

Keep Your Girlfriends   157

Make Time for Yourself   171

Don't Take It All So Seriously   185

Don't Wish for Someone Else's Problems   203

Darla's Favorite Resources   208

A Few Final Thoughts   212

Acknowledgments   215

INTRODUCTION

Hi, my name is Darla Shine. As I begin to write this book I'm sitting at my kitchen island arguing with my seven-year-old son, Connor, about how sloppy his spelling words are. My four-year-old daughter, Hannah, is in the family room watching *Doggie Daycare* for the sixth time today. I made lamb chops for dinner. I just scrubbed the greasy frying pan, and my husband still is not home. It's 7:45, and while everything in my house right now is a bit crazy, I wouldn't change a thing.

I know there's a lot of excitement today about being a desperate housewife, and it really makes me angry—so much so that I decided I had to write this book. I think it's just a shame that society looks down on at-home moms and the true art of homemaking. It's really a wonderful opportunity to be able to be at home with your kids, creating a supportive, loving atmosphere. I can't imagine what could be more important.

The dog is barking now, and the kids are running in circles around me. I'm going to try to write this book at my kitchen island in this chaos—I have no other choice. This is my life. It's a bit hectic right now. You know what, though? This is motherhood. Kids run. Kids are wild sometimes. Some days are worse than others. But I brought these children into this world, so I'm here to raise them. I want to scream sometimes, but mostly I just laugh. I hope I'll be able to finish this book in the midst of this insanity.

Hold on for a bit. I have to go bathe the children.

OKAY, I'M BACK. I put the kids to bed and I straightened up for a few minutes. I like everything to be clean and nice before my husband comes home.

Now, that sounds old-fashioned, right? Well, what's wrong with that? After he's had a long day at work, I like to greet my husband looking good, with my life under control. When he walks in the door I'll be ready to sit with him and have a glass of wine and hopefully some romance. Plus, the truth is that I don't want him to see me sweat. I don't want him to think for one minute that I can't handle all this—because I can.

So, do I think I'm superwoman? No, but I can write this book because I'm every woman. I had a big career that I left to be home with my kids. I attend black-tie affairs with my hubby at night, and the next day I'm in my jeans picking dog poop off my lawn. I've had my highs and my lows. I've been really fat and really skinny. I've been depressed, I've been happy. And thank God, I'm happy today.

But I remember when I was a mom on the edge, too. For a long time I really thought I was going to have a nervous breakdown. Being home with two small children and having a husband who was never at home was exhausting. Motherhood was harder than I thought it would be, and marriage was more work than I expected. I was lonely, scared, and most of all worried that I couldn't pull off the whole at-home-mother thing without becoming a woman with no identity, a woman whom no one found interesting, or worse yet . . . the frumpy housewife that I dreaded becoming. I felt really sorry for myself, but I didn't want to feel that way. I prayed every day that I would snap out of it.

Finally I did. I found a way to get my act together. One day I woke up and realized that these truly are the best years of my life. Being with my babies was a gift from God. Having a strong marriage was worth fighting for. I was given a new opportunity to embrace marriage and motherhood. It was a gift that I now know was invaluable. I got myself on a schedule. I made up some simple rules for myself. I got my husband on board. And now I thank God every day.

I now know so much, and I want to share it all with moms everywhere who think they're on the edge. Help is here. I'm going to get you on track. It's time to stop acting desperate and start getting happy.

There are a few things that you'll need to become a happy housewife. You'll need respect; pride; confidence; passion; friendship; a clean, beautiful home; and, most importantly, a close relationship with your children. I'm going to show you how you can achieve all this—without having to be perfect.

You'll find that once you start bonding with your home, spending time with your kids, enjoying the pleasures of a healthy marriage, and paying attention to your needs as well, your life will transform. You can have it all. Well, you can almost have it all. You'll have to give something up—for me it was my career. Sorry, but you need to get out of the office and back into the house if you want to hold it all together. Otherwise, something will suffer. What is it going to be? You, your marriage, your children, your home? Your job isn't worth it.

I should state right now that this book is not for full-time working women. There are plenty of books out there for working moms, and of course there's *Working Mother* magazine. I have yet to see *Stay-At-Home Mom* magazine; maybe I'll start it! For whatever reason, being a stay-at-home mom—a housewife—has gotten a bad rap. I want to put an end to that. I want women everywhere to call for a movement to send women back home.

To all my girls out there who did choose their families over their jobs, I'm writing this for you. For us. Together, we can bring back the art of homemaking. We can take pride in being at home. We can show the world that we can look good, have great sex lives, be interesting, run our own businesses, be creative, and find ways to make money without leaving our families for twelve hours a day. Let's admit once and for all that we like to make crafts, we like to bake, we like to be home, and deep inside we're happy that our husbands are out there working and we're not.

Like the rest of the housewives in the world, I want my family to be healthy and happy. I want a beautiful home full of tradition, memories, and happiness. I want to grow old with my husband. And through all of this I don't want to lose my sense of self.

So, join me. If you truly are ready to embrace marriage, motherhood, and homemaking, I'm going to help you. This is truly the most wonderful experience of our lives. Let's stop acting desperate and start enjoying it.

Please Stop Whining!

Let's stop acting like desperate housewives

Snap out of it!

Shut up!

Count your blessings every day

Please, I cannot take another minute of hearing women talk about how desperate they are. What's going on? When did it become fashionable to be an out-of-control mother on the edge? When did it become in style not to have your act together? When did it become popular to be a desperate housewife?

What on earth is going on in this society when one of America's highest-rated shows promotes drug abuse, adultery, statutory rape, murder, bad mothering, and the basic breakdown of family values?

When did we women decide that we wanted our image to turn from happy home-maker to desperate housewife? Is this really the image we want?

Do you think I'm overreacting? I don't think so. I'm sick and tired of hearing women who have it all bitch about how hard they have it and how much more they want. I'm so disgusted with it all that I had to sit down and write this book. I want to help all women out there who think they're desperate to stop, smell the roses, and wake up before it's too late—before you lose your marriage, before your children are ruined, before you destroy yourself in the process.

Let's Stop Acting Like Desperate Housewives

I want mothers everywhere to dismiss this horrible image of desperation and come together to promote the image of the happy housewife, the mother who has her act together, the woman who has a strong marriage, the mother who wants to be with her children, the woman who is proud to be raising her family.

You can do it. The first step you need to take is to stop whining. Stop complaining. Stop it now!

We really are tired of hearing how hard your life is. We're all struggling to do the best we can. All moms are in the same boat. We all want the best for our children. We all want to keep our marriages alive. We all want to be happy. We all want to raise our families without losing our minds. Hey, I know it's hard. It's a struggle. I work hard every single day to pull it all together, but you know what? I make it work.

I do think some of us work harder than others. I see a lot of moms who are at home but not really there. These are the moms who are out all day shopping, playing tennis (well, I do this, too, but there's a limit), and going to the salon, and yet they never seem to have time to play with their kids, cook a meal, or clean their own house. I have noticed that the women who have the big houses, the housekeepers, and money to burn are the ones who seem to complain the most.

I know. I used to be one of them. I had a housekeeper, I was going to the salon at least twice a week, I was going out every weekend with my husband, and mostly I was turning into a lazy, self-absorbed blob. I didn't know it then, but looking back now I can see how much time I spent complaining about my life, whining about being a mom, and trying to keep myself superbusy so I wouldn't have to face the dreary monotony of everyday mommy/housewife life. I left my career to be with my children because I thought I had no other choice, and I was full of resentment. I refused to let myself feel like a housewife. I rejected the idea of motherhood. I told myself it was all temporary, like a criminal sentence—and I was doing my time.

I began to get disconnected from my home and my kids. I hired sitters—any teenager

I could get my hands on—to come over to my house just so I could get out for a pedicure. I was so desperate one time that I brought home some twenty-two-year-old girl I met at the beauty shop to play with my daughter so I could take a nap. I got so lazy that if I spilled some jelly on the counter I wouldn't even wipe it up—I would leave it for the maid. I was out of control.

The saddest part was that even though I had all this help, and my husband could afford to give me new clothes and other pointless crap, I still wasn't happy. I still felt on the edge. I still couldn't appreciate any of the blessings in my life. All because deep inside I still felt as if I were too good to be just an at-home mom and housewife.

Then one day I said this to my mother. I called her while she was on vacation in Florida and asked her when she was coming back home, because I was exhausted and felt on the edge. I remember telling her that I wanted to drive my truck into a tree. I was being sarcastic, of course, but while I was whining and complaining, she began to flip out. My mother told me off good. She said that I had a lot of nerve. What the hell did I have to complain about? I had a beautiful house, two healthy kids, and a husband who loved me, and I should shut up and count my blessings. My mother proceeded to remind me about my cousin who was struggling every day to pay her bills, the woman in my play group who just died of lung cancer, my friend who had six miscarriages, my neighbor who had to deliver a stillborn baby. She told me that even though she and my father had me when they were only eighteen and lived in a tiny apartment with no money, no car, and no family support, she was happier than I was, and she never complained. She also reminded me that being a good mother didn't just mean being at home—it meant getting involved, playing, cooking, taking care of my home, and taking care of my husband. All of which she said I was slacking on. She said that my friends and I were a bunch of spoiled brats, and we all should know how lucky we are.

I pretty much blew her off and hung up on her. I rejected what she said, because what the hell did she know anyway?

Later, her words started to sink in.

I thought about my circle of friends, most of whom are financially secure, have strong marriages, and have household help. And believe me, these women take care of themselves. Every day they go to the gym, to the salon, to lunch, and to the country club. I started to think about them, about all of us. Who was on antidepressants? Who was unhappy in her marriage? Who was cheating? Who was miserable?

Each one of us had something to complain about. We were all a bunch of whining, moaning, nagging, selfish . . . yes, brats. And really, what the hell did we have to be unhappy about? Nothing. I started to feel really guilty. This wasn't who I wanted to be.

Then, a few days later, a friend and I were sitting on my patio drinking margaritas while both of our babysitters sat fifteen feet away from us playing with our baby girls. I looked over, and I realized then that I was a jackass. I was making myself sick. I had become the kind of woman I totally despised. I had become so lazy and selfish that I wasn't even playing with my own daughter—I was paying someone else to do it. What kind of mother was I? What kind of wife was I? I had become a selfish psycho-bitch who was completely disconnected with her children and her home.

My mother was right. My generation of women were a bunch of self-absorbed, money-hungry women who needed a severe reality check.

I felt ashamed. I was very sad, for me and for my family. I went upstairs that night and prayed.

I HAVE NO idea how it happened—I'm going to call it divine intervention—but the next morning I woke up and found a lump in my left breast under my nipple. I decided I was cancer-ridden and probably near death. Amazingly, I was just weeks away from getting breast implants. All my girlfriends were getting new boobs, and I wanted some, too. But, all of a sudden, all I wanted was my own boobs. All I wanted was my body, intact, cancer free. The plastic surgery seemed so ridiculous. God was testing me, and I knew it.

I had to wait two days for my appointment to have the lumpectomy. During those days I agonized about my children being left on this earth without me. I was sick to my stomach. I thought about all the women who had died of breast cancer, and I wept for them. I prayed with all my heart to live to raise my children to adulthood. That is all I wanted. Just to live. Just to be with my husband and children. All my priorities changed.

When the surgeon removed the "little fibroid cyst," I vowed never to forget how precious every second of life is. I realized then that what was most important to me was my family. I wanted to raise my kids. I wanted to be in love with my husband. I wanted to enjoy every second of my life, and I finally began to embrace the opportunity to be at home with my children as a blessing instead of a punishment. My "near death" experience (yes, I'm exaggerating, but hey, you never know what could happen) made me realize how fast my children are growing up. While my boob was in bandages and I had to lie on the couch, I asked my husband to bring me the photo albums of my babies' births. Looking at them, I vowed to stop being a jerk and start getting my act together. I made a decision right then and there that I was going to be the best wife I could be, the best mom I could be, the best homemaker I could be—and I decided that I was going to be great at every part of it.

I let my housekeeper go. I started cleaning my own house. I started vacuuming, scrubbing toilets, and mopping floors, and you know what? I was actually enjoying it. I remember telling one of my best friends that I was getting rid of my housekeeper because I needed to bond with my home. She thought I was crazy, but it was the best move I had made in a long time.

I started cooking again. I prepared huge dinners and invited family and friends. I organized my house. I got on the floor and started playing with my children again. I put myself on a schedule. I started working out. I stopped eating all my kids' leftovers. I started reading everything I could find about homemaking, from raising brilliant children and cooking great meals in minutes to spicing up your sex life.

I then got rid of the babysitters—well, mostly. My husband Bill and I still do have date night every Friday night (more on that later). I started playing with my children, spending most of my time with them and taking them with me on errands. Now, I work my schedule around my children's schedule. I want to be with them.

You know what? I've learned an amazing thing: that I could do it all without going crazy, without getting desperate, without losing my mind. I found out that I could still be me without losing me. I learned that I could still keep my own identity while being a mommy. I pulled myself together, snapped myself into shape, stopped complaining, and started enjoying my life as a happy housewife. I realized that I have a really good gig. I found out that I'm really good at this whole housewife/mommy thing.

In fact, I have this whole mommy thing running so smoothly that I decided to help my girls out there. You can do this, and I'm going to show you how.

Now my whole outlook is different. I'm a homebody. I feel sorry for all the women out there who are still trying to hold on to this image of being supermom. It's just impossible. I now know that I can't have it all. Something has to give. I've finally let go of my ego, and since then I finally have freedom. I've let go of all the demands and the expectations society put on me to be this perfect woman. I cannot be her, and I choose not to be her. I don't want to work ten hours a day. I don't want to get on the commuter train at 5:00 A.M. in a blizzard. I don't want to break the glass ceiling. I now know exactly what I want. I am desperate no more. I am proud to say I'm a happy housewife.

I think days go by when I don't leave the kitchen. I look forward to snow days when the children and I are stuck in the house. I look forward to rainy days playing games when we're all together. I look forward to cooking dinner, making a school project with my son, and dancing on the coffee table with my daughter. I realize now that this was truly my dream: to be here, a mom, a homemaker. I feel really lucky to have this chance to realize that I have only one shot at this. I'm not going to let this moment pass without enjoying it thoroughly.

Hey, before you know it, girls, we're going to be old, with kids who live far away, flabby bodies, fixed incomes, and when we look back on our lives we're going to wish we could live it all over again. When I look back, do I want to see myself at the salon getting a manicure, or do I want to see myself on the floor playing blocks with my children? I know what I want . . . do you know what you want?

Snap Out of It!

I just can't get over the fact that suddenly women everywhere are referring to themselves as desperate housewives. At the PTA, at Starbucks, on the playground, moms are chatting up a storm, proudly calling themselves desperate and talking about how much they love this show. Maybe I'm missing something. I don't know, but to me these women of Wisteria Lane really don't look desperate at all. They look pretty good.

How many of us live on such a picture-perfect block? And what about the figures on these housewives? Most moms I know are constantly struggling with their weight, starving themselves, on the latest fad diet, at the gym every other morning, and wishing they looked as good as these ladies.

So, one mom is on the edge with her boys running wild. Well, who the hell isn't? My kids drive me crazy on a daily basis, but I haven't resorted to stealing a supply of Ritalin from my neighbor's kid.

I guess I'm just out of style. Now that I'm happy to be at home raising my family, I realize there's no support out there for at-home moms. I realize there's no positive promotion about housewives. This makes me really angry.

When did being a good mom and being proud to be at home with the kids go out of fashion? Instead, it seems to be in style to be out-of-control, selfish mothers who are sluts. Oops, sorry. That was harsh. But really, are the women of Wisteria Lane who we should aspire to be? Is this really the image we want to promote? Let me fill you in. It shouldn't be prestigious to be a desperate housewife. It sets a negative stereotype of who we are. A show that portrays mothers as drug-using, bitter, vengeful whores is not a good image for us to aspire to. Yet, each week the ratings show that women from all walks of life are getting a kick out of seeing their sisters in such desperate situations. Why?

I want to know when it became acceptable to cheat on your husband. When did the forty-five-year-old crowd start getting tattoos across their backsides, showing thongs under their low-rise jeans, and trying to dress like their teenage daughters? What's going on? I think it's all ridiculous.

I like to look good. I'm going to teach all of you moms how you can be a hot mama a little later on, but some of these women are going too far. I say this not because I'm jealous. I'm thin and I could wear what I want, but this new fad of women who could be grandmas trying to act twenty is just too much.

Enough is enough. Grow up. Act your age, ladies.

Shut Up!

These women on Wisteria Lane have it all. They really should shut up and look around. Their children are healthy. They have food to put on the table and obviously plenty of money to spend on designer clothes and lingerie. They have nice, expensive cars; cleaning women; and landscapers. They all have the luxury of being at home with their children, and at the end of the day they all have men who want to curl up next to them.

But these women living on Wisteria Lane are a bunch of whining, spoiled rotten bitches. Thank goodness I'm not like them anymore. Thank goodness I snapped out of that dysfunctional state years ago while my kids were still babies, and thank goodness those desperate housewives are fictional characters. The women I'm really worried about are the ones who tune in each week and rave about how much they love the show and how much they can relate to the Wisteria Lane girls. It's these women I want to talk to. I want these women to look around at all the heartache in the world. Look around at all the illness. Think about how bad your life could be.

How easy it would be for everything you have to slip away. In an instant it all could be gone. I know what that feels like. The fear that you may lose it all can be life-changing.

I wish this for every desperate mother: to realize how lucky you are. In fact, reports show that housewives today are better educated, more informed, and more involved, and they hold most of the spending power in their relationships. So, I ask again, where is the desperation? We have it pretty good, girls. Being a housewife does not mean you're on house arrest.

I hear many women complain that they feel trapped at home, that they need to have more freedom. A lot of women I know say they're attracted to the show because it gives women freedom to admit that being a mom really sucks sometimes. The show gives women the freedom to admit that they, too, are screwing around or just not happy. All of these issues used to be taboo. I admit that. And, yes, I think it's a good thing for women to be able to talk to other women about their lives and to share and support each other. But that isn't happening on Wisteria Lane.

Those women are all phony. One burned down her friend's home, for goodness' sake, and kept it a secret. The slut who is screwing her seventeen-year-old landscaper (and should go to jail for statutory rape) isn't telling her girls in the hood her dirty little secret. The other wife, whose husband is into S&M, isn't going to talk about that over coffee, I assure you. Oh, and didn't that same mom cover up her son's hit and run? How's that for some good old-fashioned family values? How's that for prime-time TV on Sunday night? Remember the days when Walt Disney aired on Sunday evenings and introduced a real family movie? We have come so far. Is this the type of freedom we want? I think not.

Here's another thing we can thank the women on Wisteria Lane for: bringing to our attention what whores housewives have become. I cannot believe it, but a recent study showed that 50 percent of housewives are cheating. At first glance at this number you can joke and say, "Hey, it's about time the wives caught up with the husbands," but here is a double standard for you: Is this the behavior of a mother? Is this the example we want to set for our daughters and sons?

Why are we as a society not frowning upon adultery? Is this a goal that women are trying to achieve, screwing around as much as guys? It's just disgraceful.

I recently read an article that stated that women are leaving their husbands, their families, in pursuit of a hot romance. Maybe these women are not sexually satisfied. I'll talk about that later. Maybe housewives are cheating because their husbands aren't satisfying them—and yes, I think women, especially moms, do deserve to have hot, steamy sex—but since when has it become acceptable for the housewife to screw around while her husband is at work? You can have a hot, passionate, healthy sex life. But you should have it with your husband. I think cheating is bad, whether it's the husband or the wife. But now to have it spotlighted on television in prime time on a network owned by Disney is just beyond me. Not only cheating, but with a minor. What the hell is this?

How about promoting healthy sexual desire inside of a good marriage?

Hey, don't get me wrong. It's hard work to keep the passion in your marriage alive. But my husband and I still have it. We make it a priority. I'm going to show you how you can have hot marital bliss a little later.

So, where's the freedom, really? It's inside the woman at home watching. The freedom that all housewives in America now have to openly say yes! My marriage sucks. Yes! My husband is into kinky sex. Yes! Finally, I can admit I'm miserable.

Now we can finally be open about our sex lives, how bad our kids are, the debt we're in, our family arguments. You name it, we can finally lay it all out on the table. This is just great. Let's all air out our dirty laundry.

I just have this to say: When you act desperate, you look desperate. How about this? Instead of popping drugs, cheating on your husband, or hiding in the office all day, go home, embrace motherhood, hold on to your babies, raise your kids yourself, nurture your marriage, and build a safe, beautiful home for your family. It's a lot of work, but it's the most rewarding thing you'll ever do.

Take it from me. You don't have to be desperate. You can be happy. I'm going to show you how to do it. By the end of this book you'll feel great.

Count Your Blessings Every Day

It really breaks my heart to think about all the time I wasted feeling sorry for myself. I pray to God to forgive me. I pray that I can one day forgive myself for all the times I wished I had more, for all the times I lost my patience with my children, for all the times that I complained about my life, and mostly for all the times that I wished for someone else's life. Thank God I snapped out of it. Now it's your turn. Think about how lucky you are. Before you feel sorry for yourself for one more second, please stop and smell the roses. You're here. You're a lucky woman. Just the fact that you have life is a miracle. Please, I beg you to embrace it. Savor every moment.

Save the act of desperation for when you really need it. God forbid the day comes when you really are desperate—if you or a loved one has an illness, or you're in financial ruin, or worse than that.

You have it pretty good.

Let's face it, girls, most of us do have it pretty good. We don't have to work. We can stay home, go shopping, take a nap, go to lunch with the girls, take the kids to the beach, bake a cake, volunteer, take up a hobby, work part time, start a home business, whatever we want. I think being at home gives us a lot of freedom to really enjoy life and all it has to offer. Does spending your day in an office really sound fulfilling? Honestly? Come on, you know I'm right. We have a pretty good deal, girls, and it's about time we started to brag about it. The next time you're at a cocktail party with working girls who think they're hotshots, how about saying to them, "Oh, I'm lucky enough to be at home—thank God I don't have to work my ass off at the office anymore. I'm so lucky that my husband takes care of me and I get to be with my children." Start bragging.

My husband just came by and asked me my plans for tomorrow. I said I was planning to take the kids to the beach. He said, "I wish I were you." He has a point. I'm glad to be me. I have a good life. Thank God I'm aware of how good I have it. I'm happy to say my life is under control and I'm *not* desperate.

I think a lot of women feel sorry for themselves because they have to run the house, care for the kids, and hold the family together. Stop and think the next time you're at the table in the morning drinking coffee in your warm, cozy kitchen. Think how lucky you are. Be glad that you aren't stuck being the breadwinner.

Being home in a warm, comfy house floating around in your pajamas and furry slippers while sipping coffee as your babies play on the floor and your hubby works hard to pay for it all is not desperation. Grow up! Shut up! Count your blessings!

Be Proud! Being an At-Home Mom Is the Most Important Job

You had these kids: go home and raise them

I walked away from it all, and you can too

The feminists sold us a raw deal

Why you just cannot have it all

It's time to lift up our spatulas and demand some respect

A conversation with my seven-year-old son:

"Connor, how would you feel if Mommy got a job like Daddy and went to an office every day?"

"No, no way. You already have a job."

"What is my job?"

"Taking care of us. Mom, being a mom is an important job because you help your kids out when they need help, you keep the house clean, and if you had a real job you would never have time to play with us."

"Are you proud of me?"

"Mom, I am sooooo proud of you. (Hug) You cook really good macaroni and you're beautiful."

You Had These Kids: Go Home and Raise Them

Out of the mouths of babes. But I think it gives a clear indication that children, especially very young ones, want and need their mommies to be home with them. I do have to give credit to the women on Wisteria Lane; they're all home raising their children. But, to all of you who are out there working full time, unless you would starve or end up out on the streets, literally, I have to ask you, what job do you have that is so important that you would allow yourself to drop off your six-week-old baby at full-time day care? What career do you have that you would allow your teenage children to come home to an empty house day after day? I don't know what I find more upsetting, a baby in day care or a latchkey kid.

Obviously, this does not apply to the women who are divorced or single moms who have no other choice but to leave their children. My heart goes out to them. I'm sure those women wish every day that they could be home to care for their kids. I feel so sorry for these women, because finding adequate child care is almost impossible, and when you can find it, it's unaffordable.

All of us moms who do have the luxury of being at home should be doing more to help other moms, the truly desperate ones, the ones struggling to find decent, affordable child care. I think about that woman in the news who kept her child in the backseat of her car every night with a flashlight, crayons, and coloring books while she worked. How quickly the media jumped on that story, how fast everyone pointed fingers at her, how fast they wanted to punish her. What that woman needed was help. She was a single mother who barely made minimum wage, and was trying to keep herself and her kid off welfare. So sad. What was she supposed to do? I don't know the answer, but I think we should put good child care at the top of the agenda or help women stay at home when their children are young.

I'm calling on the women who started the feminist movement to get on the ball and start helping mothers in distress. But they're not interested in women who aren't highly successful career girls. They don't care about us housewives. More on this later.

Right now I want to talk to all the moms out there who can afford to be at home with their children. Women who have husbands who can support their families. Women who are leaving their babies for eight to twelve hours a day. The moms who are struggling trying to juggle their careers and their families. I have to ask you: What are you doing?

I know you feel guilty about your choice to continue working your way toward that glass ceiling, and I do agree with you that it totally sucks that you have to give it up for your family, but that's just the way it is. I'm sorry. Unless you're the breadwinner and your hubby is going to stay home and raise your babies, you should do it. You brought these little people into the world, so go home and raise them. It's not your mother's responsibility. Even if you have supernanny Jo Frost coming into your home, it's not her kid, it's yours.

I know this is really hard to hear. But the truth is, I think, down deep it lets a lot of women off the hook. Many of us are torn between our careers and our families. We work very hard, only to have to give it all up.

What choice do you have? This is really what you were meant to do. If you made the choice to get pregnant, you should make the choice to stay home with that baby if you can afford to, and I think most of you could afford to.

I know I'm making a lot of women angry. How dare I call career moms selfish? How dare I say women belong at home with the kids? How dare I suggest moms who are at home with their kids are better mothers than moms who work full time outside of the home. Well, sorry.

I Walked Away from It All, and You Can, Too

I had a career. I was making a lot of money. If I had stayed, I would really be making a lot of money now. Just as in all families who make a choice for the mother to stay at home, we made our priorities. So, maybe you'll have to give something up. Maybe this year you won't buy a big-screen TV. Maybe you won't go to Bermuda. Maybe you'll have to downsize your home. Things might get tight. But isn't your baby worth it?

Just the other day I saw a woman walk out of a full-time day care facility holding a very small infant, about two months old. It was after 6:00 P.M., and she clearly was saying hello to him. "Mommy missed you sooo much." Then I saw her pack that little sweetie into her big, expensive BMW.

If you're working for all these extra material things and leaving your babies in day care, I feel sorry for you.

If you're working because you're like many of my friends who say they just can't be at home all day with the kids, I feel sorry for your kids.

No at-home mother will tell you it's all glory being home with the children. In fact, being home with your babies is the hardest job there is. I know. I've been on both sides of this fence. Being at work fourteen hours a day is a breeze compared to being at home raising children. That is why so many women stay in their careers, because they just can't cut it. You have to be strong, confident, and selfless to be able to give up your career, give up your identity, give up a piece of yourself—all for your family's best interest.

It's the at-home moms who deserve the respect of this nation. The women who raise good people to lead the world. This is the most important job there is.

Ronald Reagan said he would have never aspired to greatness if it weren't for his mother. The same is true of Bill Clinton, George H.W. Bush, and Jimmy Carter. All these men said that it was their mother who laid down the foundation for their spiritual beliefs, their dedication to become something in life, their desire to help others. So, what would Nelle Reagan think of the new trend of these selfish mothers of today? I wonder. Back in Nelle's day, women were home raising their children. Nelle and her friends weren't out getting tattoos across their backsides, whining about how hard they have it with their kids, and complaining about their husbands. Back then, mothers were happy to be able to feed their boys.

Happy they weren't being sent off to war. Happy their husbands were employed. Think about your grandmother and how hard she had it. No dishwasher, no dryer, and I'm sure a lot less money and fewer options than you have. But I think our grandmothers really were happier than we are. Deep in their souls they had more peace than we do. They knew their place was in the home, and they took pride in that.

Oh my God! Did I just say that? A woman's place is in the home. Yes, I think it's true. I'm proud of that. I'm proud to be a mom. I'm proud to be a housewife. What is better than this? I get to wake up with my children, play house all day, and spend my husband's money.

There was a time after I gave birth to Connor when I was depressed. I'll tell you the horrid details of that later, but as I lay on the couch with my son I thought about all my friends who were still working in my field, moving up the ladder, while I was a fat, lonely new mother. I truly felt sorry for myself.

When I took Connor to the park I wanted to scream across the playground, "I'm a television producer, I'm smart, I'm not just a housewife."

I had just signed a three-year contract on a new morning talk show with a six-figure salary. I had an expense account and car service. I was thirty and thrilled to be at such an exciting time in my career. I worked very hard to get there. About three months into my dream job I discovered I was pregnant, sooner than we had planned. I was happy to be expecting, but sad that I had to leave the new position that I loved so much. And I resented my husband, who didn't have to make this choice.

But I walked away. I quit. I was devastated. What could I do? I knew I could not leave this innocent little creature with a soft skull in the hands of some stranger for ten hours a day. I didn't have parents living close enough for babysitting. And, in the field I was in, we were talking about ten or more hours a day at work, and that was just not an option for me.

Over the next year at home with my new baby I was really miserable. I was annoyed that my husband was moving up the ladder while I was stuck at home. I was tired and lonely, and I felt as if I had nothing in common with those housewives on the playground. So, I isolated myself with my baby. I tried my best to get through the day by pretending that this was all just temporary.

Then one day I sat down in the rocking chair to nurse Connor. I turned on the television, and it was as if Dr. Phil, who was on *Oprah* that day, was speaking directly to me.

A woman had written in to the show saying that she resented her husband because they were both attorneys but she left the practice to be at home with her babies, and it was driving her crazy that he was so successful while she was just a housewife. Dr. Phil said something like this: "What's stopping you? You made the choice to be at home; if you wanted to be working, you would be. You could work part time from your home; it's your practice. You could bring the kids with you if you wanted. You have to stop resenting your husband and start figuring out what you want."

He was right. I was full of baloney. I chose to leave work. I wanted to be at home with my son. Dr. Phil set me free from my own ego. I was finally able to admit to myself that I had no intentions of going back to work and that it was time for me to give up that identity. I was a housewife. Why, though, did I feel so ashamed for so long?

I know the answer now. It's because our society has looked down on motherhood as an option for a career. As if it isn't good enough for you to be a mom, to be a housewife. My entire generation of women were raised to be more than housewives. It was engraved into our brains at an early age that we could finally be something. Our sisters before us—oh, and I'm going to talk about them in a bit—opened so many doors for us, and now we were expected to step up. We had to take our places in the workforce. We were expected to be something. Aspiring to be a mom, to get married, was not something we said out loud.

The luxury that our mothers had as girls was that they knew that even though they would go to college, most likely their main goal was to meet a man who could take care of them so they could stay home. I think our mothers were far more fortunate that us. They weren't plagued with this unrealistic burden to be superwomen juggling career, marriage, and family. They knew being home raising a family was the most important job, and they took pride in that.

It's such a shame that society has put this terrible pressure on women—this ridiculous notion that we can work full time, raise a family, keep a happy home, and not lose our sanity in the process. If you try to do all this, you surely will become desperate.

When our mothers were home, they weren't ashamed because all the women were at home back then. There were no mommy-and-me groups, because the whole block was a mommy-and-me group. The moms were home, and the kids were outside playing. I never had a playdate as a child. My mother never had to arrange playtime for me. We played with the kids on the block, all our mothers were at home, and all our dads were at work. There was only one girl in the entire neighborhood whose mother worked full time. Jean's parents were divorced, and her mom worked in the city. This was really unbelievable to the rest of us. It wasn't what we were used to.

Looking back now, I realize that I grew up in a suburban American bubble. I can remember all the cars pulling into the neighborhood at about 5:00 P.M. when all the fathers came home from work. I remember that clearly. We all went home to have dinner with our families. We were excited to see what mom cooked for supper. My mother was always there. All my friends' moms were always there. We never came home to empty houses. We could never get away with anything because our mothers were there to smell us, look in our eyes, and ask us forty questions. I think the reason my entire group of friends and I grew up without any big incidents is that we grew up this way. I believe the traditional family setting with mommy at home is important. How come our mothers knew this but a lot of women today are rejecting this idea?

Our mothers were at the bus stop in their housecoats, at the grocery store with their curlers in their hair, and you know what? I think they were more secure with who they were than we are. My mother was always proud to be a housewife. She never wanted to work a day in her life. She always said being a mom is the hardest job there is, and the most important. She was right.

I think I was able to walk away from my career because of the way I was raised. It just seemed like the right thing to do—to be home with my children. Plus, from the day I got pregnant, my mother annoyed me every chance she got about quitting my job when Connor was born. "You know you have to quit your job. You have to watch your baby. If you leave him with a nanny, she'll kill him; if you leave him at day care, he'll catch meningitis, or worse, he'll get a flat head and be ruined emotionally for life because no one ever picked him up off those filthy sheets in those decrepit cribs, yadda yadda yadda," she would say every time I spoke to her. At the time, my parents lived in Florida and I was in New York, so my mother helping out with my baby was really not in the cards. Bill was never going to leave his job, and let's face it, I would never have him at home raising my baby. Yes, he's capable, but I would be insanely jealous. I wanted to be with my baby. And even before my mother was nagging me to death about what I was going to do, I always knew deep down in my heart that I would work for a while and then go home and raise a family. I just didn't realize what a struggle it would be for me.

I can remember when I was in my twenties, fresh out of college, thinking I was the hottest thing going. Just starting out in my career, I thought I was unstoppable. I wanted to be editor of *Cosmopolitan*. I wanted to be a reporter. I didn't want to be like my mother. All she ever wanted to be was a housewife. She was perfectly happy in her plight. I couldn't believe that she could be so content without having a career. I asked her once, I remember I was about twenty-four, "Mom, didn't you ever want to be something?"

She said, "I thought I was something."

"No," I said, "how could you be happy just being a housewife?"

"Why, what's more important than taking care of your family?"

Looking back now, I see that my mother was very wise at a young age. She knew what she wanted. She was perfectly content. She was proud of her life.

But my mother never raised me to believe that I could only be a housewife. My parents gave me the confidence to believe that I could be anything I wanted. My father said, "Go to college, have your career." My mother said, "But then go home and raise your babies. You can always go back to work when they get bigger."

I don't think either of them knew how conflicted I would be. It was easy for my mother to say, "Hey, go become something and then give it all up to be a mom." Our mothers have no idea how they have burdened us with liberation and equality. It's an enormous responsibility to live up to. It's exhausting. It's a shame that so many of us are still trying to juggle everything, and it's no wonder so many of us are getting desperate in the process.

I'm angry that I wasted so many days of my new baby's life on that emotional roller coaster, struggling with the knowledge that I chose motherhood over my career, conflicted over the fact that I was no longer of value in this society because I wasn't a big career girl. I felt less valuable being "just a mom." I was worried that I wouldn't be able to break back into the industry when he got older. Instead of embracing new motherhood, I was worried that I was turning into my mother and that I would never be more than a mother and wife. Now I know how ridiculous those feelings were. Now I am stronger, smarter, older, and, most importantly, I am wiser. I now know that there's absolutely no job more important than being at home raising your babies.

I wish now that I could turn back the clock. I would give anything to hold my son Connor again when he was just a newborn. I daydream about my babies and how they smelled—and in those moments I become a desperate housewife. I'm desperate to hold on to every second I have with my children and my husband, to every lucky second that I get to live this life that God gave me.

Now I would never dream there could be anything better than being a mother and a wife. It's an honor. It's the career of a lifetime. Benefits include unconditional love, joy, happiness, and laughter. Perks include sex, hugs, kisses, someone to cuddle with, someone to grow old with, and grandchildren to visit. Expectations include loss of sleep, high expenditures, no privacy, and a lifetime of worry. Salary, you make the budget. Make sure you give yourself a bonus from time to time.

The Feminists Sold Us a Raw Deal

When I was deciding what I would write, I knew that I had to take on the women behind the feminist movement. While I'm grateful for all the work they have done to help us all gain respect in the workplace, I'm annoyed that they've dropped the ball for women at home.

In college I was a huge feminist. I was even registered to vote under some feminist caucus. I volunteered at homes for battered women, I took women's studies courses, and I protested an album cover that had a woman sitting in a meat grinder. I loved it all. I thought being a young woman was the greatest thing on earth. I felt strong, I felt empowered and smart, as if I could take on the world. I was grateful to the feminists, especially my professors who helped me realize that I could become anything.

Once I had my big office with my big job and my big paycheck, I thought I was a big shot. I could go to the "in" parties, hang out with the "in" crowd, and I was "in." It felt great. But then, when I left my big career to be at home with my little baby, I quickly learned that I was "out." At parties with my husband, my feminist sisters were no longer interested in what I had to say because I was just a mom. Suddenly, I went from being interesting to being an outcast.

One day I was smart and funny, and the next I was stupid and boring. None of my big-time career sisters wanted to hang out with me, the loser mom living in suburbia. I finally felt the stigma so many housewives were feeling. I was insensitive to it when I was working. I, too, lumped all housewives into the dumpy-frumpy category. I was just like these women—a big snob. Now that I was on the other side of the fence, I understood how much it hurt. I felt sorry for myself at first. But then I got angry.

Who the hell were these women? Why should the feminists be leading the only movement? Where were the "mamanists"?

Most of the feminists out there promoting working, career, having it all, being superwoman—they're full of it. You cannot have it all. They know it, but they won't admit it.

Why You Just Cannot Have It All

I just don't believe you can work full time, run a household, raise great kids, and keep your marriage strong without losing your mind along the way. I think something will suffer, either your marriage, your kids, or your sanity. If there are women out there who are able to do all this, I'd like to meet them. If they think leaving their babies with a nanny all day is having it all, I just don't agree.

They've sold an image that just isn't what most women want. This is why today the feminist movement has lost steam in America. Now that we have entered the work-force, now that we do have some power, now that we're liberated, now that we're better educated, we know what we want, and we're starting to leave the office to head back home.

Gloria Steinem is probably horrified to read the recent statistics about women going back home to raise their children. All the hard work of the feminists is going down the drain. Really, what is the point of working so hard toward a career that isn't conducive to raising a family?

Why isn't NOW, the National Organization for Women, fighting to help more women work from home? Why are the feminists not forcing more companies to promote work-share programs with other moms? More importantly, why are the leaders of the feminist movement not supporting real choice? Not just the choice for reproductive rights, but the choice for women to work or not? I want feminists everywhere to really support their sisters, all of them, especially the ones with the hardest job of all—the at-home moms. These are the women who really know how to juggle responsibility. These are the women who know how to get a job done. We at-home moms are not lying on the couch eating bonbons. We're educated women, we hold the spending power in our families, we're raising the future; and to all you career girls out there, until you have walked in our shoes, you better get out of the way. You won't be able to keep up.

At a party about a year ago I overheard a group of women who worked in advertising talking about how they're tired of soccer moms trying to control their industry with all their boycotts and calls to the networks and politicians. "What do they know anyway?" one woman said. I wondered if they were talking about the same soccer moms who are juggling their kids, their husbands, their households? They know nothing? You wish you were among us soccer moms. You would never survive a PTA meeting with your big mouth and bitchy attitude. You better listen up. We soccer moms make up a huge voting power, we're the ones with our husbands' wallets, we have spending power, and you better start giving us some respect.

These single women out there who snicker at us at-home moms think we're uninformed, soap opera–watching hags who vacuum all day and have no idea what's going on in the world. Well, I have something to tell this society. The at-home moms of today are better educated and more powerful than those of any other generation. We have started small businesses, have found ways to work from our homes, and are getting stronger as a group—and we're not going to take any more abuse.

It's Time to Lift Up Our Spatulas and Demand Some Respect

Our country supposedly stands for family values. Why is the role of mother so undervalued? A mom runs a home, keeps a budget, stays on schedule, meets deadlines, and is responsible for raising people who will run the world. Ask any woman who works full time as a CEO to step into your shoes and try to be successful managing four boys under age seven and see how she cuts it. Find any businesswoman who has devoted her life to her career and see if she could hold up in your house for a week. She doesn't have a chance. This is why so many women hide out in the workforce all day—it's much easier to be in the office than to be at home with the children. As you know, I've been on both sides, and working is a piece of cake compared to being an at-home mom.

I'm sick of hearing women ask, "Are you an at-home mom or do you work?" Well, I answer, "Yes, I work very hard. . . . I am a mom."

I'm calling on moms everywhere to hold your spatulas high, and together let's take back our positions as family matriarchs. Let's fight this stupid image these desperate housewives are giving us. We're not desperate at all.

I want us happy housewives to reclaim our position. Let's start a movement to go back home with our babies. A movement to say out loud, "I'm at home with the kids." No more of this hiding behind the "domestic engineer" title at cocktail parties. You don't have to feel ashamed.

Let's be proud that we put our families first. Be proud that we're holding it all together, making it all work. This is what I wish for all of us: to feel proud and to demand respect from society. We happy housewives are the ones raising the future—isn't that worthy of some respect?

Think about how you run your life. Think about how beautiful you are as a woman. Think about the possibilities we all have. We have so much power.

If we could stop whining for a few minutes, think about what we could achieve as a group. Women hold most of the spending power in their households. Women are educated. Women have the babies. We're not our mothers. We're not afraid to speak up and fight for our rights. If only we could join together, we would be the strongest voting power in this country. If we could just stop the backstabbing and support each other and the choices we make. If we could open up and share life together, it would be a beautiful thing. If we could all be girlfriends and appreciate each other for the women that we are, what a wonderful thing it would be. Just think about it.

It's the women who are smart, raising babies, taking care of their husbands, creating beautiful homes, who cook, clean, pull it all together, and do it every day. . . . It's us, the strong, happy housewives, who really are the women with power.

I can tell you right now that I have had it. There's so much we could do to demand respect. There's so much more we could do to support each other.

So, let's forget about the feminist movement and start our own movement.

You can *almost* have it all; look at me:

> *I am at home with the kids.*
> *My husband and I have a close, intimate marriage.*
> *My house is clean, decorated, organized, and gorgeous.*
> *I cook breakfast, lunch, and dinner almost every day.*
> *A couple of nights a week I get takeout.*
> *I am thin and I look good.*
> *I am not on antidepressants, and I am not stealing my friend's kid's Ritalin.*
> *I have lots of friends and make time to keep those relationships alive.*

I play tennis, go grocery shopping, vacuum, and do laundry.
And at the end of the day, I still had time to write this book.

So I gave up my career. What did I lose really? The long hours, not being there for my children, missing my daughter's recital, not getting to watch my son's first home run, all in an effort to make it to the top . . . to break the glass ceiling? No thanks.

Stop Looking Like a Housewife

Find the hot mama inside of you

Eat healthfully

Save yourself

Get moving

Research it yourself

Vitamins

If I see another mom at the mall wearing sweatpants and a big old sweatshirt, I'm going to just go absolutely over the edge. Hey, mama, what happened to you? Where's the girl we used to know? Look at you. Look at what you've become.

Am I shallow? Yes, a bit. I just want moms to realize that they can still look good, that they should *try* to look good, that being a mom is not an excuse to look like a strung out woman who just rolled out of bed with throw-up on her chest. I know you could be beautiful. I know you're unhappy about being dumpy. I know you want to be in style, in shape, looking like the woman you once were. I know you could be a hot mama. My question for you: *What are you waiting for?* You still have a lot more living to do. You have the rest of your life ahead of you. It's time—now—to take action. You need to get your act together, and I'm going to help you.

I think one of the biggest reasons housewives have a bad image is that a lot of moms have let themselves go. Admit it, girls. Most housewives are in desperate need of a makeover—out-of-date hairstyles, jeans that should have been thrown out years ago, and worst of all, what I really cannot handle, no makeup! Unless you're absolutely naturally beautiful—and ladies, let's face it, most of us aren't—*please* don't leave your house unless you at least have lipstick on. Everywhere I go—the grocery store, the school, the park—I see moms showing up looking like they just rolled out of bed. No makeup, dumpy clothes, and the absolute worst thing in the world—an oversize sweatshirt and leggings. I'll say this just once, so listen closely: *Leggings are not in style.* Big sweatshirts make you look *BIG*. Those gray drawstring sweatpants should stay on your husband.

Okay, ladies, I know a lot of you have been busy with the babies, taking care of the home and hubby, but you've got to get yourself together. I don't want to hear you say you don't have time to fuss. I don't want to hear you say you were just running out the door. I don't want to hear you say what you wear doesn't matter. What you wear certainly matters. If you look like a dumpy-frumpy housewife, that's what you'll feel like, and that's what people will think of you. You're too young to give up. You should look good every day. You deserve to look good every day. If you feel good about the way you look, it will make you feel better about yourself, and you'll be happier. I'm going to show you some easy steps you could take each morning to get out the door looking great. In just a few minutes you could bring back the woman you used to be. I know she's in there somewhere. We all want to see her again. And I'm *very* sure that your husband would like to see her again.

One thing the girls on Wisteria Lane have is sex appeal and style. We could take a few pointers from them on that note. Even when they're hanging around the house dressed down, they look like hot mamas. Gabriella is proof that you can wear sweatpants, as long as they're stylish and tight. The reason the moms on Wisteria Lane look good is, of course, that they have a staff of people working on them—but they should give you a reason to step up to bat. If you keep your hair in style with an attractive cut, and if you spend five minutes every morning putting on some makeup and a cute outfit, not only will you look like the hot mama you are, but you'll feel better about yourself—and I promise the new you will find new sparks in your marriage.

Find the Hot Mama Inside of You

Gabriella isn't a mom in real life, but her character gives us a good example of how sexy housewives can be. You can and you *should* release the sexy woman inside of you. I know she's in there somewhere—dig down deep! I'm going to force you to bring her out.

Remember when you're picking out clothes in the store that your big goal is to feel good about yourself, to be the girl you used to be. Don't hide in mommy dumpy-frumpy fat clothes. Buying new big sweatshirts is not the answer. I have two girlfriends who hide their bodies in these oversize sweatshirts and button-down men's shirts because they want to keep their big bosoms covered up. They're so self-conscious about their big knockers that they wear these tents over their bodies. All they're doing is making their upper body look even bigger. All they're doing is drawing more attention to what they're trying so desperately to hide. I urge them to shed the material, to buy a good bra and let those babies shine. I wish I were stacked like them—but this just goes to show you that we all have different body issues. We're all self-conscious in one way or another. I just read a survey in *Newsweek* that said only 3 percent of women were satisfied with their bodies after giving birth; however, an amazing 94 percent of their husbands said they thought their wives were as sexy as ever.

Women agonize about their body image even when they look fine to the rest of us. Most of my friends are struggling with one body issue or another. One thinks her nose is too big, one wishes she had bigger boobs, one wants straighter teeth, one is trying to get rid of cellulite, and I think I am too short and my thighs are way too chubby—but we're all trying to look the best we can with what we have to work with.

So accentuate, ladies. Pick your best features and use them to your advantage. I think I look good when I'm pulled together. I make a cute package. I work at it. If I let my roots grow out, if I didn't keep up on the tweezing, the fussing, and the frumping, I would be a scary woman.

We all need to work on looking good. It's a sad fact, ladies. Please don't scare us. Do your part to keep up with the rest of us. I think my group of girls are doing a pretty good job. We look cute, we're thin, we're in style, and we're hot mamas! At least we think so. We're constantly on top of each other, policing each other to make sure we don't fall off the wagon. We force each other to look good. Most importantly, we feel confident. We love our lives. We love our husbands. We're happy housewives, and that shines through.

My best friend Jill and I have a loving competition over who looks better, who is hotter, who has it going on more than the other. We're both writing books, we both have powerhouse husbands, we both struggle every day to keep ourselves together, and we push each other to be more than we expected. We often joke about how easy it would be for us to fall off the wagon, get fat, and become lazy blobs. Staying a hot mama is work. Yoga, the gym, eating healthy, staying fit, keeping a cute 'do, wearing makeup, buying the latest trends—it's a commitment.

You can do this. You're a mother—you can do anything. You're a beautiful woman. Look at how much you've accomplished. Let your beauty shine. Let your womanhood show. Release the hot mama inside of you.

Once you feel better about how you look, you'll be able to take my next step, which is to turn up the heat with your husband. When you feel like a hot mama, believe me, you'll be ready for some romance in your life. We'll get to that in a minute.

For now, let me help you get on track. I want you to go throw every piece of baggy clothing, and any item that is more than a year old, into a box and donate it to the church. Go to the store and buy some new clothes. Get your hair cut. Buy some new makeup. My mother has makeup in her drawer from 1962. Why do women think makeup lasts forever? It just isn't true—six months, one year tops. Mascara, two months—that's it. But for goodness' sake, put on some makeup. You need it, and so do I. Get started.

If you need help, look at what the women are wearing in the magazines. Real women in magazines like *More, Redbook, Ladies' Home Journal, Woman's Day*, and *InStyle*. See what everyone is wearing. You could reproduce any look within your budget. Don't wait to lose the weight, just buy a few things for now. You'll feel good, and you'll be on your way to the new you.

A lot of you are going to say that you don't want to waste money on clothes that won't fit you once you shed the pounds. I say that's a cop out. You don't have to wait until you lose twenty pounds to start looking better. While you're getting in shape you have to feel good about yourself. You need to keep your hair in style, put on some makeup, wear fashionable clothes.

I gained a lot of weight during both of my pregnancies. It's embarrassing. I gained seventy pounds with Connor and fifty with Hannah. After I lost the weight from my second pregnancy, I swore that I wouldn't wear anything unless it was tight. Not crazy, slutty tight, just form-fitting, tailored clothes. I never wanted to look like a hot air balloon again. I was so happy to have my waistline back that I was going to accentuate it every second I could. The only thing was, I was 103 pounds and a size two when I became pregnant with Connor, and when Hannah was a year old I was still twenty pounds overweight. I realized that I might never see 103 again, and I doubted I would ever be a size two again. I had to face the facts and I had to move on. I had to accept my new mommy body. I was a few sizes bigger, with more padding on my hips, but I decided to make the best of it.

I think we all go through a post-baby stage when we turn into house-frump hags. It's okay to go through this. I'll give you six months to lounge around in your pajamas with your new infant. Then you have to get your act together. Six months after having Hannah I decided I had to bring Darla back from the abyss.

I started working out and eating better, and even though I was nowhere near my pre-baby weight, I went out and got my hair highlighted, my eyebrows shaped, and a bikini wax, and I bought some new makeup and clothes.

I discovered that once I started wearing cute clothes I wanted to get the old me back. I keep my closet stocked with T-shirts and turtlenecks, all spandex/cotton blend, and jeans and slacks in various colors. I can throw on a pair of beige slacks and a white long-sleeve T-shirt and I am out the door. This is a cute look that anyone can pull off. So, before you even lose the weight you can still look good. No matter how big you are, you'll still look thinner in clothes that are not bulky, baggy, or big. I don't even own a pull-over-the-head sweatshirt—yuck! I don't want to look like my husband. I want to look like me. Get rid of all these horrible sweatshirts. Unless it's a fitted zip-up hooded girlie sweat jacket, forget this look.

You don't have to spend a lot of money, either. You can look great on a very small budget. Target has some really cute clothes that copy the latest runway trends. Talk about cheap—Old Navy always has shorts, T-shirts, and jeans on sale for next to nothing.

Kohl's, JC Penney, and Sears all have gotten their act together, and I've noticed they're carrying a lot of really cute clothes that are very affordable.

If you're lucky enough to buy expensive designer digs, good for you. I think it's really a waste of money. I splurge on my hair, on accessories, and on shoes and bags. I love shoes and bags, but for everything else—I call it the stuff in between—as long as it's tight and the latest style, you're set. (Just a side note—as I write this, Hannah is sitting in a toy stroller next to me screaming at the top of her lungs and insisting that I push her around the house. It's 8:44 P.M. and she should be in bed. Bill is still not home. Hold on while I give her a spin. . . . Okay, I'm back.)

Once you feel confident, once you allow yourself to feel pride in being a housewife, once you decide that you're not going to be a schlub anymore, once you decide to release the hot mama inside of you, there will be no stopping you. Now that you feel proud to be a mom, show it off. Be confident. Make sure you look good. Show off your voluptuous body. Be proud of whatever stage you're in. When Oprah was heavy she still dressed nicely, she still did her makeup, she still had her hair done. She was proud of who she was no matter what size she was wearing. Look at her now.

I'm not saying that you need to attend the science fair decked out in high heels and a skirt. In fact, there are quite a few women who overdo it. I think this whole trend of forty-year-olds trying to dress like their daughters is just stupid. I see women with their boobs pushed up to their necks with way too much cleavage showing. I see women, who I know could be grandmas, wearing tight low-rise jeans and slutty spike heels. I was with my daughter at a birthday party—in a gym, no less—when one mother showed up wearing six-inch heels and her size triple Z implants hanging out all over the place. Ladies, when you try to look seventeen, you really look desperate. Who are you trying to impress? Really, you desperate mothers, you're not teenagers anymore. Face it, deal with it, move on, and be the best forty-year-old you can be.

That doesn't mean you have to run off and get a total body makeover at the plastic surgeon. I see many women now who look completely different than they did a year ago. New nose, new boobs, new ass, new cheeks, and so many cat eyes staring at me. . . . Hey, I'm not saying I'm against doing some tweaking when you really need it, but ladies, let's not go overboard. I know women who had really cute B or C cups trade them in for a double D. I also know women who have their faces scraped every few weeks.

I just don't understand all these moms in their thirties who are going for Botox injections and getting dermabrasion every month. When did we become this shallow? I think it's sad that we're so terrified of growing older, so insecure, and so desperate to hold on to our youth.

A friend of mine, a plastic surgeon in New York City, has perfected a technique for a mini-facelift. She performs it on women in their late thirties before they start to look bad, so the idea is you get it in your thirties, your forties, your fifties, so you always look good instead of waiting until your face is about to hit the floor. I thought it might be something to consider one day when my neck is hanging down like a gizzard, so I went on *Good Morning America* with her and told the world that I was considering the operation, but I was thinking in ten or twenty years. I shouldn't have gone on, because now everyone who saw that segment thinks I had my face done.

I think my skin looks great right now. The problem is that I get no credit for my skin looking good. At my high school reunion this past summer, a few of my old girlfriends who haven't seen me in twenty years said, "Wow, that face lift really works, you look great." I think it's hysterical that these girls thought I had the operation. I'm going to take it as the best compliment. I get a lot of compliments on how nice my skin looks, and I am lucky to have good wrinkle-free genes, but my real secret is that I don't overwash, I slather on the moisturizer every night, and I wear a hat on hot summer days. I keep my face out of the sun.

Remember, girls, all the plastic surgery in the world isn't going to keep your husband in your bed or send friends flocking your way. Be smart, funny, and confident; be a real woman, a great friend, a good mother; read a book, become interesting, and love who you are and the body God gave you. Once you start feeling good about yourself, your life, your marriage, and your home, your inner beauty and your spirit will shine. This is why it's so important to me to help housewives find peace in their lives. Feeling fulfilled and satisfied will motivate you to be the best mother, the best wife, the best friend, and the best homemaker. Feeling confident is the best pick-me-up.

Some Tips for Looking Like a Hot Mama

1. *Buy a few cute hats, and on bad hair days throw one on—suddenly you go from strung out to fashionable.*

2. *Buy a bunch of cheap, cute, clear sunglasses, and on days when you are tired and have circles under your eyes, throw a pair on and you'll look like a movie star.*

3. *Remember to accessorize. You could pick up gorgeous beaded jewelry, big fun bracelets, and dazzling earrings. Any plain outfit transforms once you accessorize.*

4. *Don't forget your belt. A cute belt really does make the pants. I see so many moms wearing tucked in tees . . . how cute would you look with a beaded belt?*

5. *Stop wearing sneakers. Unless you are at the gym or going for a long walk, a cute pair of sandals or mules is the way to go. Remember, a small heel is sexy. Jeans and sneakers . . . frumpy; jeans and a wedge sandal . . . hot mama.*

6. *Please don't wear those tees or sweatshirts with photos of your children on them. Nothing says dumpy housewife more than this.*

Eat Healthfully

Please start eating healthier. There are a thousand diets out there, but I hate the word *diet*. Just follow what I do—don't eat junk, nothing processed. I am a liar, of course. I eat some things that I shouldn't once in a while. But mostly I control myself. Not only for calorie intake, but to simply eat healthier. Salads, greens, vegetables—these provide antioxidants that help you fight cancer. If you eat healthier food, the weight will start to come off. Stop eating starches, eat absolutely no fast food, eat small meals every two to three hours, and drink water all day. And of course, no snacking on the couch at night.

I know it's hard to pick a plan. I believe a few diet plans are better than others. I think for the most part, though, if you're not stupid, you can lose weight and stay thin. First of all, stop eating your children's leftovers. I know, I know, I used to scoop whatever was left on their plates right into my mouth. We all hate to waste food. But you have to. You're older, your metabolism is different now, and you just cannot get away with eating anything you want anymore. I know, it totally sucks!

Listen, I can bitch about this because I have been on both sides. I told you how much weight I gained with both of my pregnancies. The weird thing was that I was Skinny Minnie my whole life. Up until I became pregnant with Connor at age thirty I had been a size two. I could eat an entire pizza and drink it down with two chocolate milkshakes and not gain an ounce, but then I was pregnant and everything changed. I was so fat that I had to put Balmex on my inner thighs because I was getting blisters from them rubbing together. My face was so distorted that when I went to visit my parents in Florida they didn't recognize me when I got off the plane. I lost all the pregnancy weight within a year of giving birth. Well, almost all the weight. One year up, one year down is what I say. But today I'm still fifteen pounds heavier. I weigh 118. I have been a steady 118 for about two years now. My body has settled at this number; it seems to like it. I'm not sure I'll ever be as thin as I was ten years ago, but I feel confident, I think I look good, and, most importantly, I feel healthy.

It took a long time for me to realize how important it is for me to be healthy. I think many of us take our health for granted. We all make mistakes that affect our health. Many of us are so goal oriented, so set on being thin, that we forget about the important things like nutrition. Like me, so many women become obsessed with losing their baby weight that we just starve ourselves, and this is the absolute worst thing we could do.

If you eat a healthier diet you'll feel great, lose weight, and ensure a better life for you and your family. I've often noticed in grocery stores that it's the heavy women who are buying a whole lot of junk. The other day when I was grocery shopping I noticed the woman in line in front of me loading a ton of processed snacks onto the checkout counter. Bags of chips, dips, beer, cookies, cheese, frozen snacks, fried chicken, and ice cream. I looked at all her items, and there was not one fresh vegetable or piece of fruit— just cans of veggies and fruit. She was about eighty pounds overweight, and I wanted to shake her. Her son came up behind me to stand near his mother; he was about twelve years old and at least twenty pounds overweight. I was so angry that I wanted to smash my cart into her big fat ass. But then I thought to myself, is it possible that she just doesn't know about nutrition? Is it possible that she was raised to eat this way, and now she's passing on her bad habits to her son? As her food moved down the conveyor belt, I began to load my fresh organic lettuce, tomatoes, apples, bananas, spinach, broccoli, wild salmon, bottled water, kettle chips, and tofu ice cream onto the belt. I hoped she would look over and that it would inspire her to eat healthier. She didn't seem to notice; she just paid and left the store.

I thought about her all night. I think what made me so annoyed was that she was turning her son into a man who would have weight issues throughout his life, that if she fed him some fresh fish with sautéed spinach instead of the frozen fried chicken dinner, he might even enjoy it. I wished she would give him a fresh peach instead of the canned peaches full of sugar. I wondered if she knew that what she gives her young son now will affect his health for the rest of his life, that the food he eats now will literally build the body he needs to sustain his manhood.

Maybe I'm too neurotic about it. My son cried the other night because he said there was no good food in the house. Why does everything have to be organic? Why does everything have to be healthy? He was hysterical. You know, he sees his friends with bags of Doritos at lunch, and he wants that too. So I do give in and give him chips, chocolate, and cheese doodles, but in moderation, and only after he eats something healthy. "Eat a handful of blueberries and I'll give you a handful of Doritos," I'll say. I'm also big on hiding the good things that they eat. I make a lot of smoothies, and I throw yogurt, fresh fruit, and milk into a blender with ice and tell them it's an ice cream shake. The same works for me. I throw spinach, beets, apple, and carrots into the juicer and drink it down. Make sure you're getting your raw fruits and veggies every day, and make sure your children do as well.

Keep the junk away from your children. Remember, if it's not in your house, your family won't eat it. The other day I made a big pound cake with chocolate icing from scratch for my mother's birthday, and since the cake was so big there was a lot leftover. After the company had left and the kids were fast asleep upstairs, I was sitting here writing and staring at that cake across the room. I wanted to dive in. I had a piece earlier for dessert, but it was still making me crazy. I knew if I didn't get rid of it I would eat the entire cake right then and there. I put it into a freezer-safe Rubbermaid container and placed it in the garage refrigerator. I'll defrost it over the weekend when the children will be home with friends to enjoy the rest of it.

Keep a bowl full of fruit on your counter and healthy snacks available for the children. I always have cut-up carrots and ranch dressing dip, which they love. They also like to eat pretzels, and Paul Newman has a nice selection of healthy organic pretzels on the market. I also keep raisins, cold cuts, and cereal available for snacking. If my children get overly hungry, they become really irritable. I have dinner ready at 5 P.M. because by that time in the day they're starving. If you make them eat a nutritious breakfast, lunch, and dinner, they will eat less and not want the junk during the rest of the day.

Save Yourself

One day when Hannah was about two years old I fell asleep while I was giving her a bath. It was about 4:00 in the afternoon, and I just could not stay awake. Every day, all day, I was tired all the time, and every muscle in my body ached. I had contracted Lyme disease right after I gave birth to Connor, and at first I thought it was coming back, but the tests proved negative. I can remember feeling as if I were a neglectful mother because my son was begging me to play blocks with him and I just couldn't muster up the energy even to stay awake. I had to have my mother come up from Florida to stay with me because I just had to sleep.

Of course, when I went to a male doctor, he said, "Oh, of course you're tired. You're a new mommy." All he could do for me was to diagnose me with fibromyalgia, an autoimmune disorder that causes muscle ache and fatigue, but there is no effective treatment. After a few more months of feeling lousy I decided to take matters into my own hands. I refused to be a blob. I began to research everything, and I read it all: websites on health, holistic healing, nutrition, and women's issues.

What did I discover? My body was desperate for nutrition. For about a year I had been consumed with being thin again, and I realized that my entire diet consisted of coffee—about seven cups in the morning, along with my beloved bagel from Best Bagels in Bayport, then more coffee throughout the day, and at night I ate whatever was left over from the children.

I knew I had to change my diet, so I started reading about nutrition. I knew my body lacked vitamins. I started popping various vitamins and herbs. I knew my body needed more exercise and sunshine. I threw the kids in a double jogging stroller and started running. I visited a wonderful Ayurvedic doctor, Dr. Kumuda Reddy, who really saved me from having an anxiety attack, and I started practicing the ancient Indian art of healing, Ayurvedic medicine, which focuses on treating the physical, mental, emotional, and spiritual health of the individual. So I began to meditate, to breathe better, to begin yoga classes, to massage my body with oils, and to change my diet. I needed to rid myself of all toxins and parasites, and I did this simply through changing my diet. There are many good internal cleansers you can purchase at health stores today, but I just started to eat raw greens every day. And on the advice of my friend Dina, I started to juice. I began to juice watermelons with their rind and drink it daily. Then I added wheat grass, barley grass, and beets, and soon enough I began to enjoy more energy than I had my entire life.

I could go on and on about nutrition and holistic healing, but I'll do that in another book. I'll just say it's really disgraceful that women are blown off by the health care industry the way we are. It really makes me sick that there's not better diagnostic testing for female cancers, such as ovarian. For now I'll simply beg you to take your health care into your own hands, and start by changing your diet and exercising. Whatever you do, get moving. Whatever you do, eat breakfast every morning—it's the most important meal. And for goodness' sake, whatever you do, please do not pass your stupid eating habits on to your children. Change now, before it's too late.

For breakfast I have either scrambled eggs, a bowl of cereal, or granola with fruit and kefir. Let me tell you about kefir. It's a kind of drinkable yogurt that can be found in your health food store, and it cured me of years of irritable bowel syndrome. It's a probiotic that helps line your intestines with friendly bacteria that your body may be lacking. I'm lactose intolerant, and the kefir does not upset my stomach at all. I used to get stomachaches daily, but I have not had one in over a year with the kefir.

I eat a lot of eggs. I buy organic free-range eggs, and I believe they're a perfect food, full of nutrients. Since they're a protein, I feel good eating them. I sauté some fresh spinach and tomatoes and throw in some eggs, and I love it.

I still have my bagel at least once a week. Now I eat only one side, and I toast it with some ghee, or clarified butter, which is much healthier for you than regular butter. You can find it in your health food store. If I eat a bagel in the morning, I make sure I stay away from breads during the rest of the day.

I always keep frozen muffins and bananas on hand, and if I have to rush out the door I grab one to go. This is important. I have several girlfriends who eat badly because they have nothing in the house. So, make sure you always keep some frozen bagged fruit on hand or some granola in an airtight container in your pantry—and frozen bagels, of course, but control yourself. Just because you have it doesn't mean you have to eat it all at once.

Don't worry so much about eating. I eat all day, whenever my belly tells me to feed it. I just eat small amounts of real food, not crap. What is real food? Here's how I can tell: Does it have a paragraph of ingredients that I can't recognize? If so, I don't eat it. I try to eat foods that are basically in their original form. Get it? Eat fresh produce, greens, all veggies, all fruits, and you'll be set.

Hold on, it's 11:00 P.M. and I'm starving. I'm going to make myself a bowl of cereal. Forget that don't-eat-after-7:00 P.M. nonsense—if you're starving, eat. Just don't be stupid. I am eating fat-free organic whole wheat cereal: one gram of fat, no saturated fat, and 170 calories with milk. I use lactose-free organic milk. I feel fine about eating this snack because it's healthy, or at least healthier than a lot of other things that are in my pantry right now. I know there are coconut macaroons in there, but I'm staying away. I had two this afternoon as a snack, and that's it for today. They're loaded with fat.

Let's face it, it's easier to be fat. You have to fight to be thin. It's worth it, though, don't you think? You can do it. I know it's a struggle. Give up all the junk. Just give it up.

The one thing I just cannot give up—or should I say I just refuse to give up—is my morning coffee. I just love it. It's a habit, I think, but I tried to give it up and I decided to forget it. I have given up many other things, but I'm not giving that up.

But be proud of me; I've knocked it down to only two cups each morning and none the rest of the day. I do have my tea with honey in the afternoon. That's during my relaxing time, when I have my macaroons or a piece of chocolate. You can have some of your favorite treats; just don't eat the entire box of chocolates. My mother will sit in front of the television and snack all night. My father is always eating. He's very thin. Maybe it's in my genes not to get fat. Or maybe I have my parents' eating habits. My mother always forced us to eat. We never skipped breakfast as kids. I never skip breakfast because I wake up starving.

I'm exhausted. I have to get to sleep now.

GOOD MORNING, GIRLS. Yes, I have my nice cup of joe in my favorite mug, ahh. It's not really morning, though—it's about 11:00 A.M. I've had a busy morning.

I was on the phone most of the morning trying to explain the difference between real food and fake food to my girlfriend Cathy, whom I have known since the third grade. She's always struggling with her weight, and while she's never been heavy, she always wants to be thinner. (She's on Weight Watchers now, which I think does work—my husband Bill lost thirty pounds on it. He also went to the gym three times a week.) Anyway, I am trying to teach Cathy to try not to eat anything man-made. I told her if she eats food in its original form—not screwed up by humans—she can eat as much as she wants and all the weight will come off. Salads, melons, beans, vegetables, even a baked sweet potato. See the difference? Eat a sweet potato, not a bag of chips. Eat an apple, not an apple strudel. There's a cute little book that I like by Susan Powter. Remember the *Stop the Insanity* (New York: Simon & Schuster, 1993) diet girl from about ten years ago? Well, she looks better than ever, and a few years ago she wrote a new book, *The Politics of Stupid* (Seattle: Crone, Inc., 2002). She taught me how to eat real food, not a bunch of processed junk. She gives oatmeal as one example. She says everyone thinks oatmeal is a healthy food, but did you ever hear of an oat tree? Her point is to eat only foods that haven't been altered by humans. I agree this is difficult to do—as you know, I love my cereal—but if you mostly do what Powter suggests, you'll soon reap the benefits.

I know it's really hard not to eat anything prepared or packaged, but try to eat as little of it as possible. Hey, about half an hour ago I ate a cupcake. But for lunch I'm going to have a huge salad that I made with chopped apples, tomatoes, mixed greens, and bean sprouts. For breakfast I ate two scrambled eggs and a slice of tomato with a slice of wheat bread.

I told Cathy, and I'm going to tell all of you, that I absolutely love Jorge Cruise and his new book *The 3-Hour Diet* (New York: HarperResource, 2005). There are a few books that I'll recommend to you, and this is one of them. I think he's right on the money. You can go to his website and check him out at www.jorgecruise.com. He promotes what I believe. Eat small amounts of healthy food every few hours to speed up your metabolism. He also says something that I just love—that you need to exercise only a few minutes a day.

Get Moving

I absolutely *hate* to exercise. I hate having to go to the gym. I hate having to be there at a certain time. I hate how all this working out crap interrupts my day. I would much rather be reading or cooking or, of course, eating. But it's just a fact that there's no way to get around it, because if there were I would have found it. You have to exercise.

Up until about two years ago I never worked out a day in my life. But once I hit thirty-five, I started to notice that somehow my body had shifted around. Everything had moved slightly; it began to sag, and clumps started to form. Yes, I still looked good in clothes, but when I took them off it was scary. For the first time in my life I saw a dimple on the back of my leg. For the first time I had flab under my arms. For the first time I had saddlebags. And this was absolutely what put me over the edge—for the first time I had love handles starting to pop out over my jeans. That was it. I went to the gym and got a personal trainer. Yes, it was not my favorite pastime, but you know what? In only three months my body was toned up and I looked great. I even went to a black-tie dinner wearing a slinky skin-tight gown without any stockings, underwear, or bra. Everything was in its spot and sticking up perfectly.

But like many moms out there, I soon fell off the wagon. Yes, in fact, I just ate another cupcake. While it was organic and only a few calories, I still shouldn't have eaten it. I haven't been to the gym in a year. I have a good excuse—we moved, and now I'm writing this book. I'll start with the trainer again as soon as I'm done writing. I have managed to stay thin, but my body is getting soft again. Now I have many dimples and lumps on the backs of my legs. But this year was a busy year, so something had to go on the back burner, and it was my backside.

It's unrealistic to tell women they have to get to the gym every day or even three days a week. Some of us just cannot do that. It's realistic to tell moms out there that they have to watch their weight, stay as thin as they can, and get moving however they can. So just because you cannot make a 7:00 A.M. spin class or an 11:00 A.M. workout with your trainer, there's plenty that you can do right from your home.

When Connor was an infant I put him in the baby carrier and wore him while I did deep knee bends and lunges. When Hannah was small I put her in the stroller and walked into town almost every morning, although I was getting a grande Mocha Frappuccino from Starbucks, which was probably defeating the purpose since it has so many calories. But you know what? It didn't matter, because my body was moving, my heart was pumping, I was in the fresh air with my baby, and it was good for both of us.

You can get moving every day from your home with your children. Go out and play basketball with your kid. Run around the yard with your dog. Get into the gym, play tennis, ride bikes with your kids, take a walk with your hubby. But get off your ass.

Exercise right in your own living room. I own a ton of exercise tapes, and I'm really hooked on this Mari Winsor Pilates tape. You could check her out at www.winsor pilates.com and have a workout on your family room floor while the children do their homework. Kathy Smith is also a favorite of mine. She has a gazillion tapes, so grab one and get sweating. Another workout book that I really recommend is *The Ultimate New York Body Plan* by David Kirsch (New York: McGraw-Hill, 2005). He talked me out of getting liposuction when I was really desperate. I was contemplating sticking metal rods into my backside, and then I read Kirsch's book, and he says you don't need liposuction, you only need to exercise. It made me feel like a real jerk, and it got me off the couch and doing lunges while I watched television. I have an exercise ball (I use an 18-inch size), and it works great. You can order one at www.megafitness.com. I also have the Bowflex and an elliptical machine. I try to get on those machines at least three times a week, but I have to admit it doesn't always happen.

While you watch television you can do squats, ride a stationary bike, or throw your children onto your feet. Yes, I leg-lift my daughter Hannah up and down about thirty time each night. She weighs thirty pounds, and it's a good workout for me and a fun ride for her. To do this exercise, grab your child, lie on your back, hold their hands, put your feet on their chest, and lift them up and down. Find anything you can do during the day to give yourself a little workout.

I recently read Mireille Guiliano's book *French Women Don't Get Fat* (New York: Knopf, 2005), and just the other day I saw the author on television. She said that in France women don't go to the gym. They don't obsess over being skinny. They just eat good, small, healthy meals, and they walk a lot. I love that way of life. We should all follow that advice.

The most important thing to remember is not to be stupid. I know a lot of women who have become truly desperate trying to become thin. The fact is that unless your body is naturally that way, trying to get and stay unrealistically skinny is just too much work and impossible to keep up with. The only way to do it is complete starvation or excessive exercise, and you'll ruin your health in the end.

One of my friends starves herself to stay thin. She's at an unrealistic size zero. Another friend hardly eats and lives on a diet of cigarettes and Red Bull. Every woman I know has some trick to stay thin, or should I say, some shortcut. I tell these girls all the time that what they're doing is dangerous, and in the end if they ever start eating normally they're going to blow up and be fat. You cannot starve yourself all day, because it slows down your metabolism. Oprah said that starving herself is what made her heavy initially. She starved for weeks to lose weight, only to put it all back on—and a lot more—when she began to eat again.

Also, we're all worried about dying of cancer and leaving our children alone, so why don't we realize that a diet with no nutrition will cause our bodies to deteriorate?

I've been sitting here writing for a while, and my body is telling me to move. My ass is starting to burn and fall asleep, so that is a clear indication. I'm going to jump on the elliptical for a few minutes before I have to pick up Hannah from preschool. I hate having to go down into the basement to do this; I feel as if I'm being punished. But summer is coming, and I need to look good, and that is the bottom line, girls.

We can keep our bodies strong, lean, and looking good. Look at Diane Keaton at fifty-nine, Susan Sarandon at fifty-eight, and Tina Turner at sixty-five. We still have a lot of years left, and we're going to be thin, we're going to look good, we're going to be in shape—and we're going to be hot grandmas!

Research It Yourself

It makes me crazy when a mom takes whatever her pediatrician says as fact. Why should she? We know our babies. We are the mommies. We know better. The fact that this person is a physician doesn't mean he always knows what's best for your child. Last year, right after he had mononucleosis, Connor broke out with a horrible rash. His thighs were covered with big purple and white pimples, and it was disgusting. It lasted for months, and he was diagnosed with some wart disease that was probably brought on because his immune system was weak. I took him to several dermatologists, and the best they could do for him was to burn off the warts, which, of course, I was not going to do to a seven-year-old. I research on the Internet for days, digging deeper and deeper until I found some women in Poland or Germany. I explained what I was going through, and they suggested a homemade remedy. I soaked Connor in it, and within two weeks his rash had cleared up. I took him to his pediatrician, showed her his legs, and told her about the remedy. She couldn't believe it. It's a bit radical, and I'm not sure my girls out there are ready for it because, let's face it, we can be pretty uptight. Anyway, I did my own research, I found a holistic way to heal his skin, and he hasn't had one of those warts since.

Second-guess your doctors. You know your body and your child's better than the doctor does, so get second opinions. Do some research. The Internet is a wonderful tool, and there's so much information out there that you can be knowledgeable about almost any condition when you walk into that doctor's office. I think these physicians often blow off moms as emotional, and they don't think we have a clue about anything. You show the doctor that you are informed, that you deserve respect, and that you are not going to be bullied.

I recently read a tragic story. A woman was taking her two-week-old baby to the pediatrician, and she had a knot in her stomach—she could just feel that something bad would happen. The doctor was about to give the baby that ridiculous new shot with five different vaccines inside. (It's called the five-in-one shot, and the vaccination is supposed to protect children against diphtheria, tetanus, whooping cough, Hib, and, for the first time, polio in a single shot.) I think this is too much for one newborn to take.

When the mom questioned the doctor, he told her, condescendingly, that he had to give her baby this shot or the authorities would be notified. What the hell is that? I wish I had been there with her; I would have stuck that shot right up his. . . . Well, anyway, you know how this story ends. That shot was too much for her little baby to handle, and he died that night. Of course, the doctors attributed his death to SIDS (sudden infant death syndrome), but let's use our common sense. Speak up, moms. Do some research. Don't give your child any shot, any medicine, anything at all without reading about it and knowing your options.

When I first had Connor, I was stupid. I read all the baby books, but I didn't know about the important things. I didn't know I could split up the vaccinations so that he wouldn't get three things at once. I didn't know that some soy was genetically altered, so when I thought I was progressive by giving him soy milk, I was probably doing more harm than good.

By the time I had Hannah I was ready. I did my research. I learned that New York state law says that I have the right to give birth the way that I want, that I didn't have to have an IV during labor, that I could eat if I wanted to, that I could sit up if I wanted to. I had choices. I didn't vaccinate Hannah right away, and I made her new pediatrician, whom I loved, split all the shots so that she was given them months apart from each other, when she was over age two. I do support vaccines, but not for babies who are so small that their little bodies just cannot handle these viruses.

I have been doing research on health, holistic healing, and nutrition since I became pregnant with Hannah. Ever since I cured myself of fibromyalgia and the trauma my body received from Lyme disease and Connor's birth, I feel empowered. I realize now that our health and that of our loved ones really lies in our own hands. You cannot depend on your family doctor to save you. You have to save yourself. You, mommy, are the warrior, and you have to protect your family.

I cannot take it when I hear these desperate mothers whining about their children having recurring illnesses such as sore throats, allergies, and other viruses without even bothering to do any research on them. I met a woman in the doctor's office one afternoon who was telling me that her little girl kept getting sore throats and ear infections, and the doctor wanted her to have a tonsillectomy. I asked her if her daughter was perhaps allergic to something, maybe dairy products? I learned that she hadn't done any research of her own, hadn't gotten a second opinion, and hadn't visited an allergist or nutritionist. Hey, I feel bad for this mother, and I don't want to judge her. I know it's torture to have a sick child, and I'm sure that she was truly desperate for some relief, some answer for her child. I didn't give her any advice; it wasn't my business. But I urge all of you to be smart moms. Don't take your doctor's word. Do your own research. Read all that you can on your child's symptoms and diagnosis. Be an informed mom.

It seems too obvious to have to say it, but if you have any question about your illness or a particular course of treatment, you should get a second opinion. I know a lot of women who were on their way to surgery based on the opinion of one doctor. That is all it really is—an opinion. Nothing is fact, and I don't care what any doctor says—get a second opinion, or even a third, and from physicians in different practices. Two physicians from the same practice agreeing on something is not good enough for me. One of my pregnant friends was told by her OB/GYN that her baby was severely disfigured, with no brain development, based on the results of her amniocentesis. He then brought in his partners, who all agreed with the results. Together, they urged her to have an abortion. She refused. Guess what? Her baby was born perfectly healthy.

My mother was in a lot of pain. When we took her to the hospital, the doctor on call said she probably had a bladder infection, gave her antibiotics, and sent her on her way. After a few days at home in agony, my mother was unconscious. We took her back to the emergency room, where her appendix ruptured. She survived it after undergoing a radical hysterectomy at only age thirty-nine. I was too young to really know better, but looking back I wish someone had insisted on a second opinion. When Hannah was in the hospital and I thought she had appendicitis, I asked for several doctors to check her, and when they didn't say anything that satisfied me, I insisted that a surgeon come in and feel her stomach. Once I had a few doctors agreeing that it was only a stomach virus, I felt comfortable enough to take her home. Yes, I am sure that all my doctors want to scream when they see me coming. I know they think I'm annoying. Too bad. Let's face it—our lives are in their hands. The lives of our babies are in their hands. We have to be careful. It is up to us to demand the best service, the best health care, the best options for us and for our families. So don't go for surgery—don't get anything cut out or cut off—until you get a second opinion.

Vitamins

I'm a really strong supporter of vitamin therapy. I know many moms who are tired all the time. They walk around yawning in the middle of the day, and they never have any energy. My sister takes a nap every afternoon. Other women I know drink coffee all day to stay awake. This, I think, causes a dehydration problem. If you don't drink enough water throughout the day, you'll become tired. I was like that, too, but I woke up once I started to change my diet and take vitamins.

It's easy to do the research yourself to find out which vitamins would help your specific problem, but I'll tell you that a multivitamin is essential. You definitely need calcium, magnesium, folic acid, and vitamin C supplements (I take about 1000 mg of vitamin C a day). I take all of them, along with cod liver oil, vitamin E (400 mg), and vitamin B complex.

I really like www.mercola.com and www.shirleys-wellness-café.com for vitamin information. I also urge you to give your children at least a multivitamin. Speak to your pediatrician. Besides a multivitamin, I give extra vitamin C—100 mg for Hannah and 300 mg for Connor. Last year Connor had a terrible case of mononucleosis, and it lasted for about two months. The glands in his neck were like golf balls, and he was lethargic. I started giving him vitamin C pills, 2000 mg each day, and after a week of that he started to get well. Within another week his glands had gone down and his energy was back. I have done a lot of research on vitamin C therapy, and I suggest you do so as well. Speak with your doctor before you start.

· STEP 4 ·

Make Your Marriage a Priority

Stop using motherhood as an excuse

Give your husband some attention and appreciation

Turn up the heat in your bedroom

Release the sexual goddess within you

Get a life!

Don't nag him to death

Now that you look good and feel great—now that you're a hot mama!—it's time for you to make your marriage a priority and turn up the heat in your bedroom.

You'll never be a happy housewife if you're not intimate with your husband. If you don't make lovemaking a priority in your marriage, you'll drift apart, and you'll become an irritable, dried-up old hag—yes, a desperate housewife. Many women I know are seeking more attention, love, respect, and sex from their husbands. Here's what I say to them: Take control and turn it around. I find that it's mostly the women who push their husbands away and aren't interested in sex who, little by little, destroy their marriages with nit-picking, nagging, and blaming their husbands for the fact that they don't have their act together. Sorry, but it's true.

I'm not saying that you have to love your husband more than your children, or give him more attention than you do your children. I'm saying there's enough of you to go around, and you have to give your husband and your marriage time and effort. The best gift you can give your children is the security of growing up in a family with two adults who love each other. Showing them love by example is one of the most valuable lessons they can learn.

I know a lot of women who actually brag about how consumed they are by their children and how their husbands are on the back burner. Hey, I know what it's like to be a new mommy. I know that unconditional love for an infant. I understand how deeply you love and adore your babies. I'm in love with my children. They're the best gift of my life. But I'm also in love with my husband. I can share my love and attention. So can you.

Stop Using Motherhood as an Excuse

You need to stop using motherhood as an excuse for not having sex. You have to stop this tired routine and wake up. Get off that couch and make a move on your man—before it's too late.

Ladies, you may think no one out there would want your overweight, sloppy husband who leaves his underwear on the floor and pees all over the toilet bowl, but I promise you there's another woman willing to jump into your side of the bed. And don't get that attitude with me (oh, let her have him), because that wish just might come true. I know a lot of women who didn't realize how good they had it until they were alone, having to go back to work full time to support their kids and not finding a man as good as the one they had.

Even if your hubby wouldn't take the bait of another woman, doesn't he deserve to have the woman he married? Doesn't he deserve to have sex? You can't *always* be too tired. Does he deserve to be the brunt of your hostility at the end of the day? No.

Oh, stop feeling sorry for yourself. You're probably mad at me because you think I'm giving your husband a free ride here and making you look like the bad one. I know he could help you out around the house more. I know he could pay more attention to you, give you more compliments, treat you like the queen that you are. I know all this. I'm going to show you how you can get your husband to do anything you want. I'm going to show you how to get him to treat you the way he used to . . . when you were first married.

If you follow my steps, your husband will be vacuuming the kitchen floor, playing with the children, and being the man you always dreamed he'd be. Better than the man that you married!

Yes, it's possible—your husband will treat you better today than he did when you first got together. However, you have to be willing to do a few things: Make the first move, swallow your pride, and throw him an olive branch. I would bet that it has been you who has been pushing your husband away. Most women become so consumed with the new baby that their husband gets the shaft. My cousin complains that now he's sleeping in the guest bedroom because his wife has moved the baby into their bed. Other husbands I know joke how they never get any sex since the children came along. These guys say their wives claim they're just too tired from taking care of the children to take care of their husbands sexually.

But remember this: Once you start making your marriage a priority and once you start having some good sex again, you'll find that you have more energy and you'll be in a better mood. So stop pushing your husband away. Forget all these years of growing apart—let's start over. Let's put having a hot, steamy, romantic marriage on our list of priorities.

Why am I an expert on this? Well, not only have I tried these methods in my own marriage, but I have my friends following these steps, and their relationships with their husbands are stronger than ever, and they're happier than they've been in years.

Give Your Husband Some Attention and Appreciation

Keeping your man happy is easy. If he's happy, you'll be happy. Just make the first move and wait and see how much he gives back. The secret is that men are simple. They want only three things in life: attention, appreciation, and sex. If they cannot get these three things from you, they will either look someplace else or become miserable bastards who annoy you every day of your life. I think you'd rather have the sweet guy that you used to know when you first got married. Well, he's there—you just have to go find him.

If you ask any of my girlfriends, they'll tell you they all love my husband. "We just love Bill"—it's all I ever hear. Of course they do; he's great. He helps with the children, he's always provided for us, he puts me on a pedestal, and guess what, ladies? Eat your hearts out—he makes the beds on the weekend and will even do a few loads of laundry (including folding and putting away). I know I have it good.

Recently, one of my friends said that she wanted to know why my husband was so attentive to me, why he was always pampering me, why he was so willing to help with the children. What was I doing to get him to do this?

I told her that I give my husband what he needs, and he gives me what I need. You and your husband want the same thing—we all do. It's *attention and appreciation*. If you give those two things to your husband, he'll never leave you and he'll never cheat on you. Men cheat because they're getting attention from some cute little number telling them how great and smart they are and laughing at their jokes. Of course, the new hot sex they're having with this young woman is exciting, but they're also with a woman who is interested in them, happy to be with them, willing to do the nasty and not complain that it's a chore. It's a thrill for men to have attention from a woman, especially if their own wives are ignoring them.

And this goes both ways. I have friends who have cheated on their husbands. Why? Not for the sex, but for the mental stimulation they got from the new love interest. Finally someone was paying attention to them, noticing how good they look, and actually wanting to have a conversation. Having someone interested in you is a huge turn-on. I always tell my male friends that they had better pay attention to their wives; otherwise, the first guy to tell them they look beautiful is going to be trouble for their marriage.

One of my close friends—married with four kids and living in a gorgeous house with a rich hubby—left it all when her personal trainer started giving her mental foreplay. That's what I call it. When a man tells a strung out housewife whose husband hasn't paid a lot of attention to her lately that she deserves better, that she looks great for having four kids, and that she's still young enough to enjoy her life, it can destroy a marriage. Make sure you give each other the attention and emotional stimulation you both need to stay happily married.

Bill and I do this for each other. We always have. Sometimes we even know that we're just saying whatever it takes to make each other happy. I tell him how great I think he is, or how smart I think he is, and he tells me I'm beautiful and that I look skinny. It goes on and on, but we say nice things and compliment each other, and it makes us both feel great. Bill knows if he wants to get me in the mood, all he has to do is turn on the charm. He knows exactly what to say . . . and it's not *I love you.* My kind of dirty talk is, "You look better today than the day I met you. How do you do it all? You're an amazing mother." And recently when we were dancing at a party he whispered in my ear, "All I want at the end of my life is to look up on my deathbed and see your beautiful face looking back at me." Now, that's romance.

You could leave this page open next to the toilet for your hubby to read. But frankly, you're the one who's going to have to make the first move. Since I'm writing to my girls out there, I'm going to ask you to initiate this behavior. Start saying some nice things to your husband. Start giving him some attention. Start giving him some affection. Believe me, it will pay off.

Last year one of my best friends wanted a new dining room set, but her husband was not opening his wallet. I told her to go home, pay some attention to him, act interested in him, initiate some romance, do some nasty deeds that only married couples should do, and guess what? Two weeks later she had the furniture—and a new diamond ring to boot.

Men are *sooooo* easy. We women are the complicated ones. If we could all just shut up a little more and watch what comes out of our mouths, I think a lot of marriages would be better. Admit it. We nag, bitch, complain, gossip, and talk our husbands to death. Worst yet, we have a habit of saying terrible things that we regret. When Bill and I first got married, we decided we would never cross the line of no return. You know what I'm talking about—saying horrible things to your husband that you just cannot take back. And this goes both ways. If you throw it out there, he's going to come right back at you.

Recently at a school function I sat mortified as a woman berated her husband in front of the entire parent association. "What kind of man are you?" she said. "Why didn't you make sure you paid for the membership? Now little Johnny [not his name, of course] will be left out."

First, she should have kept her mouth shut until she was home alone with her husband, and second, she should never have insulted his manhood. Ladies, there's just nothing worse you can do to your husband than to insult his manhood. This may sound sexist to you, but it's true. Anyway, why would you want to hurt someone you love? Why would you want to embarrass the man you love? You need to show him some respect.

In fact, you both need to show each other respect. I know couples who say the most horrific things to each other when they're arguing—cursing at each other, insulting each other, throwing the worst, deep-down secrets in each other's faces. This kind of behavior can only bring a marriage to its knees. Please, watch what you say. Please remember this is the person you married, the person who is taking care of you and your children.

Does this sound old-fashioned? Maybe it is. Respect may seem like a thing of yesteryear, but men need it, and you have to show it to them. You cannot have your husband going to the office all day running a business, feeling strong and brilliant, and then coming home to you and hearing, "Take out the garbage, jackass." You can't act like a miserable mom who has no time to have any fun with her husband. Wake up and show him the attention you gave him before you had children. Show him that you still care. If your husband feels as if he comes last in your house, that you're not interested in him, that you'd rather sleep than have sex with him, week after week, month after month, it's a problem not just for your marriage but for you. You don't want this. You want a good, loving, strong marriage full of romance and passion. You can have that. You can have it better than ever. You just have to learn when to shut your mouth.

Put yourself in your husband's penny loafers for a minute. Would you want to come home to you after a long day at work? After you worked hard to support this woman, do you want to come home to see her lying on the couch in flannel pajamas, without a supportive thing to say or five minutes of attention to give? I know many women are exhausted with a new baby, but remember your big baby. Men are babies, and they need attention, too.

So at the end of the day, even if you're exhausted, miserable, and ready to attack your husband when he comes through the door because he left his towel on the bathroom floor, try to zip it. I know it's hard. Instead, greet him warmly. Get off the couch and go over to him, kiss him hello, and ask him how his day was. Act interested in him.

Let's face it. We all want our husbands to treat us the way they did when we were dating. Along the way, the kids, the housework, and the sheer exhaustion got in the way of your paying attention to him. His job, mowing the lawn, watching the game, and being tired also has pulled him away from you. The bottom line: You both have to put your relationship first.

Now for the appreciation part of this equation. Think about your husband's ego for a minute. You need to make him feel like a man. You need to tell him that you think he's smart and hard working, and that you appreciate all he's doing to take care of you and your family. Again, a lot of women would think this is old-fashioned, but why? If you love your husband, why wouldn't you say thank you for working so hard for you?

You're lucky enough to be home with your children. Think about the pressure your husband has on his shoulders. My husband is always saying that husbands get a bad rap on TV—that they're portrayed as workaholics who don't spend enough time with their wife and children. He says women need to understand that men are consumed with guilt about working so much, but really they have no choice because the pressure of keeping the family afloat is enormous. Bill says he spends hours each day just worrying about the children and the fact that he'll miss yet another Little League game.

(Hannah just asked when I'm going to be done writing my book, because she's tired and wants me to lie with her. I have to go put her to bed; I'll be right back. . . . Okay, she's sleeping, but now Bill just walked in the door. I have to go pay some attention to the hubby.)

Turn Up the Heat in Your Bedroom

You'll never be a happy housewife if you're not having good sex. You need to have a close, intimate, passionate relationship with your husband. I'm going to teach you how to schedule your day better, and you'll have time for romance. You have to make it a priority.

I don't know how the idea got out that women don't want sex. That's just ridiculous. In fact, I think the reason a lot of housewives are miserable is that they need to release some tension. If moms were having more sex, I think they'd be a lot more pleasant in the grocery store parking lot. I always joke that I can spot a woman who isn't getting enough action. She's always complaining, she looks dumpy, and she's on edge. Sorry, ladies. But if you're having a deep, romantic, intimate relationship with your husband, you're satisfied, you're happy, and you want to look good, mostly for him. If you're feeling good, it reflects in everything about you.

And if you feel that way, think about your husband. Believe me, if you start following my steps, start to look good again, and pay some attention to your husband, he'll be cleaning the kitchen after dinner, bathing the children, and handing you his wallet, no questions asked.

Last week, I was out to dinner with about six of my friends, and they were all complaining that their husbands wanted too much sex. All of them were joking about what a chore it is and that they just don't have time for it. I was the only one who said out loud that I just cannot get enough goodie time with my husband. They were all shocked.

This goes back to my secret for keeping my husband faithful, helpful around the house, and attentive to me. I want to be with him, and I'm always after him. This makes him feel good, makes him feel wanted, makes him feel as if I am still interested in him— and in return he does the same for me.

(It's 10:35 P.M. Connor just came down, he can't fall asleep. I can't possibly start writing about sex now, let me go put him to bed. . . . Okay, now let me finish my point . . .)

You see, ladies? It's easy to keep your man happy. If he's happy, you'll be happy. If he's happy, you'll get everything you want. Watch how fast your husband will wash the dishes or fold the laundry if it means getting you into the bedroom faster.

But once you get there, you had better turn up the heat. Over the years many people use the marriage excuse to let their romance dwindle. I say it's the opposite. Over the years, after having my babies, knowing I have the document and the sacrament of marriage behind me, I feel as if I can finally enjoy a great sex life between husband and wife. So turn up the heat, jump in the sack, and start having some fun again with the man you married. I promise you'll be in a better mood tomorrow.

Let's recap. Follow these steps and revitalize your marriage:

1. *Attention and appreciation. This is what your man wants—a little attention, and for you to tell him that you appreciate him once in a while.*
2. *Bite your tongue. Don't go for his jugular. Don't tell him you hate his mother. Don't insult his manhood.*
3. *Show your husband some respect. You want it, too. It works both ways.*
4. *Don't be a nag. For goodness' sake, take the garbage out yourself.*
5. *Look your best. Try to fix yourself up a bit before he walks in the door.*
6. *Call your girlfriends when you want to bitch, whine, and complain about life. Your husband doesn't want to hear it.*

I know I'm making a lot of you angry because I'm putting all the responsibility of fixing your relationship in your lap. I know your husband can be a jerk sometimes. I just want you to understand how easy it is to turn things around. You catch more bees with honey than with vinegar. Like you, I can look back on a lot of times when my husband and I were fighting, not talking, saying things to hurt each other. I can remember wanting to pack my bags and get out many, many times. We wasted a lot of our early marriage in this immature phase. It took us both a few years to come together and make our marriage really thrive. Now, ten years later, I can honestly say that our relationship is closer than it was when we first got married. Our love life is hotter. We love and respect each other more today.

Before I move on to our next step, there are just a few tips that I think need mentioning on how you can keep turning up the heat in the bedroom. Now that you're a hot mama and in the mood, here are some of my secrets to keeping passion alive:

Touch every day. Make sure you hold hands, kiss hello and goodbye each day, hug, rub his back, sit next to him on the couch, lie close to him in bed. I know this might be hard for you to do if you haven't been close in a while, but you can start slowly. Sit down with him and tell him you've decided that you want to have a stronger marriage and want to be closer to him. Tell him that you want to make an effort to be more affectionate.

Try to have one lustful, passionate kiss every day. At the end of the day when he comes home from work, greet your husband, wrap your arms around him, and give him a nice long kiss. Count if you have to—try to make that kiss last for a good three seconds. I know you might think this sounds staged and ridiculous, and in a way it is, but I'll tell you that those seconds of connection really help you bond.

And don't just have intimacy when you're having sex. Most days you won't be having sex, and it's especially important then to have contact. If your husband is plopped on the couch with the remote, plop yourself right next to him, put your legs over his, throw a blanket over the two of you and cuddle. Make the first move. Start showing affection, and you'll see over the weeks and months that your relationship will be stronger.

Don't be a zombie in bed. Don't just lie there and wait till it's over. Your husband is a man, and studies show that men think about sex every fifteen seconds. My husband says that's stupid and untrue, but I'm not sure I believe him. I know this much—men are perverts. They like pornography, big tits, sexy women, and naughty X-rated sex, and they have been thinking about it all since they were probably fifteen years old. I'm not saying you should go out and buy a whip and become a dominatrix, but I am saying that you have got to turn up the heat in your bedroom. Why not? You just might enjoy yourself. Your husband—just like you, admit it—wants some hot, wild, steamy sex. Don't believe that you cannot have a passionate sex life if you have been married more than ten years. It's not true. You just have to work on it. You can reignite the flame. What's holding you back?

Quickies are good. Just put the kid in the baby swing, grab your hubby, and run into another room. Even a few minutes of romance will rekindle the sparks. There's just not enough time for long lovemaking sessions most days. And if you wait for scheduled sex, something always comes up, like a fever, the croup, or some other ailment that will cause your child to scream for hours and your husband to become irritated because he's desperately horny. And, ladies, let's face it, if you're not having orgasms at least once in a while, we know what a raving lunatic you are. So, forget about making love. You know he loves you, so just go screw. Yes. Grab him, have a quickie in the kitchen, in the bathroom, wherever and whenever you can. Your husband will love the new spontaneous you.

Initiate it. Your husband will love you coming on to him for once. Don't wait for him to initiate sex. Why not go after your man for once? As I told you earlier, men are like big babies who want attention and affection, so put your hand on his thigh, lean in, and go for it, honey. Shake things up a bit.

Have fun. Pull over and make out in your driveway. Jump in the shower with him. Drop the kids off with your parents and go to a hotel for a few hours. It's the ho-hum stagnation of married sex that causes many husbands and wives to forget about passion. If you start having some fun together, some laughs, and some unplanned sex, you can start feeling like the couple you were when you were dating.

Don't use sex as a punishment. Please don't. You're only punishing yourself. A lot of women I know use sex as a weapon. "Oh, I'm mad at him, so he's not getting any for at least a month"—I've heard it a thousand times. Well, who are you punishing? Sex is not a punishment. Sex is really a gift to be shared between two married people. So, keep sex where it belongs, between the two of you. When you're angry with your husband, sit down and talk about it. Resolve your issues as soon as you can. Walking around the house not talking to each other is just stupid.

Bill and I are not perfect. We do get annoyed with each other. We have had some very loud arguments. But when this happens we try to talk it out and get past it. Bill grew up in a house in which the parents wouldn't talk to each other for weeks. He always said he would never want this for his marriage. I grew up in a house where my parents would say the most horrible things to each other when they were fighting that I swore I would never do this in my marriage. So we go out of our way to talk things out. And ladies, remember, make-up sex is really great. So, if you're mad at your man, bite your tongue, think about the big picture, and try not to get mad about stupid little things that don't matter.

For goodness' sake, will you buy some sexy nightwear? Get some lingerie and throw out the flannels. I think wearing beautiful lingerie makes a woman feel sexy, and, of course, it's a huge turn-on for a man. I know a lot of women don't buy lingerie because they think it's a waste of money, but how is investing in your marriage a waste of money? You don't have to spend hundreds of dollars, just buy a couple of nighties. If it's winter and you think it's too cold to wear a satin nightgown, don't turn to those old lady flannels. There are many cute lines of pajamas today that allow you to look sexy and be warm at the same time. So, get yourself to the pj's department. Looking good in the bedroom is just as important as looking good out of it. Make an effort, please.

Court each other. Even when your babies are small, you need to make time for your husband. Get Grandma over to babysit so you can go to dinner together. Even if you can get out for just two hours, go for coffee, grab a quick dinner, flirt, talk like adults. Spending time with the guy that you love, just the two of you, is a huge release of tension. Getting out and having a few laughs over a cocktail, hearing about your husband's day, telling him about yours, away from the house, away from the kids, away from the responsibilities of parenthood is necessary for you to stay close. The important part here is getting out of the house. Take a ride, just the two of you, and reconnect. You need to do this at least once a month. Don't feel guilty about leaving the children. You deserve it. Make it a priority to keep your marriage alive.

Release the Sexual Goddess Within You

I know she's in there somewhere. I know you want to enjoy your womanhood. I know that deep down you really do want to have great sex. Why don't you just admit it? What are you waiting for? You're a married woman. A mother. You deserve a big fat orgasm. And I know this for sure: No matter how tired you may be, most women would wake up from the dead if they were going to have some hot sex and a big O. But I'm really afraid that a lot of my ladies out there aren't having orgasms. They're not being satisfied by their wham-bam-thank-you-ma'am husbands, which is why they drifted away from these men to begin with. I know women who have destroyed their lives and broken up their families just because they finally were able to have some jungle animal sex and were finally getting their first real orgasms. I read a report that only 30 percent of married women were having orgasms on a regular basis when having sex with their husbands. What a horribly sad statistic. No wonder the women at the PTA are a bunch of crazy bitches. No wonder there are so many desperate housewives. Imagine what this world would be like if men were having sex without ejaculating. Imagine if men weren't being satisfied. We would have surely been nuked by now. Imagine the hostility, resentment, and loneliness these unsatisfied moms are suffering.

You need to end this now. If you've been faking it with your husband, you need to come clean now (no pun intended) for the sake of your marriage, your sanity, and your life. Let me fill you in on a secret—men love to satisfy their women. Men actually enjoy knowing they're the one who can satisfy their woman. Your husband would be thrilled to think you're enjoying him fully. So, let him know, and do it now.

You could find a way to lie about this. One of my friends was always saying that sex was a chore and she didn't have time for it, and finally one day I asked her, "Are you having orgasms with your husband?" She said that she had been faking it since her son was born ten months ago because her mind wanders and she worries. She said that she wanted to be honest with her husband but didn't know how to approach the subject.

I came up with a plan. I told her to get rid of the children, initiate sex with her husband, and really try to allow herself to be with him in the moment. I told her that instead of faking it she should let him spend whatever time it takes to make it happen. Then, if it didn't, she should just say, "Honey, it's not going to happen tonight." If this happened a few times in a row, she should just say to him, "I think it's this new vitamin I'm taking." Men believe anything.

Then, after a few weeks, she should have sex with him and tell him they both really need to work on this orgasm thing together because she needs to have one desperately. Men love a challenge. But she had to be willing to allow herself to enjoy it.

Guess what? I just ran into her a couple of days ago, and she told me my plan worked brilliantly and she feels great. She thanked me and ran off. . . . probably to go home and have some hot sex with her hubby. Good for her!

You need to show your man what you want and how to satisfy you. Believe me, your husband wants you to be a bit naughty. It's true. You know the old cliché, a chef in the kitchen, a whore in the bedroom? Pardon me! Don't be embarrassed, we're all married women here. You can admit that you're a horny housewife. Go ahead, I know you want it. I know you want to feel sexy. Put on that little black lace nightie and maybe get some of those spiky high heels with the feathers on them. (I've always wanted a pair and still haven't gotten them!) Have a few cocktails with your husband, light some candles, turn up the music, and let the games begin. Remember, you're a hot mama, a sex goddess, a mom, a warrior, and you deserve to be satisfied. So relax and enjoy the ride.

Oh, I really am out of control.

Get a Life!

This is the one thing that I just don't understand. Why do so many women insist on do-ing everything with their husbands? I say have sex together, and that is pretty much all you need to do. Really, sometimes communicating with your husband is overrated. I have my girlfriends for that! If you want to have a great marriage, if you want to be a happy housewife, you have to get a life—a life of your own.

Be your own person. Don't depend on your husband for your happiness. You need to be happy, you need to be your own person, you need to do your own thing and let him do his.

I'll get into the whole girlfriend thing later, and why it's so important for you to have your girls, but remember, your husband is not a girl. If I were going to pick out china, furniture, or clothes, dragging my husband along would be the last thing I would want to do. Really, ladies, get a life and grab a girlfriend. Your husband doesn't want to shop with you, so let him be.

Let him go play golf or softball. Whatever his hobby is, let him do it. I don't understand this do-everything-together stuff; to me it only leads to disaster. I think it's important for a husband and wife to have their own separate interests, as well as common bonds. I don't want to horn in on my husband's day at the football stadium; I just let him go. Let your hubby take the kids. Let him have a life without you. Don't suffocate your man, or he'll run away.

Go on dates with him, keep the romance alive, and try to act as if you're still dating. If you try to do everything together, of course, you'll get on each other's nerves. Now, I'm not saying to vacation alone or anything like that. I thoroughly enjoy going out with my husband, and I would never want to go on vacation without him because we really have so much fun together. The reason we have such a good time is that we look forward to seeing each other and spending quality time together, because we don't have that much time to spend together during the week.

Right now Bill is upstairs in his office doing who knows what for the past two hours, the children are in bed watching a movie, and here I am again in the kitchen writing. In a bit, when we know the children have fallen asleep, we'll watch a movie and have a nice bottle of wine. Tomorrow Bill is taking Connor to a football game, and Hannah and I will most likely hit the mall.

Being together is great. Being together too much is a nightmare. We know a lot of men who work from their homes, and the wives all say they cannot take being home with them all day. One of my friends made her husband sell his restaurant because he was never home. Now that he's at home all the time, she says making him quit the business was the biggest mistake she ever made. Women need their space in order to run the house. Having our husbands home to Monday-morning quarterback is a nightmare. My husband is a workaholic, and you know what? It works great for us.

Don't Nag Him to Death

I have friends who go through their husbands' wallets, go through their pockets, go through their desks, and question them to death. As I've already told you, you have to shut up, stop whining, and for goodness' sake, stop nagging your husband. What your husband needs from you is for you to look good, be attentive, give him sex, be independent, and be happy.

I'm asking for a lot, right? Well, I'm not done yet.

If you think about it, I'm really only asking you to be the girl you used to be, the fun girl who didn't give a crap if your guy was a slob—you found it cute. What happened to the girl who dated a guy who went out with his friends, played sports, and had his own identity while you went out with your girls, did your own thing, and had your own life? It's amazing what happens to wives over the course of a marriage that causes them to nag our husbands over every little detail.

I've heard myself doing this. Last week I could feel myself annoying and nit-picking Bill all morning. "Why did you get bagels? I would have made pancakes. . . . Why did you dress Connor in sweats? It's too hot. . . . Why are you wearing that T-shirt? It's all worn out." I could hear myself really being a nagging bitch.

Finally, Bill turned and said to me, "What is with you this morning? Shut up already—you're being such a nag." He was right. But ladies, it's true, we have these crazy hormones, and even I cannot control myself sometimes. I was getting my period and I just wanted to attack. I couldn't help it. I could feel the edge in my gut, and I really had to take a step back.

So, I grabbed the car keys, asked Bill to watch the kids for a while, and went shopping. Walking aimlessly up and down the aisles at Target with a big coffee in my hand was just what I needed. I had to be alone. Sometimes Mommy just needs to be left alone. So does Daddy. So give each other some space.

IT'S REALLY VERY simple. Men want attention, a little appreciation, and some hot sex. Isn't this exactly what we want also? So put your marriage back on the front burner. Your children are going to be fine. You can be a great mom and a great wife. You can be a hot mama and a sex goddess. You can let your husband have some space without losing him. In fact, you should let your husband have some space *before* you lose him. Live your life together as one great adventure. Keep it fun, interesting, and exciting. Women become desperate housewives when their lives become boring, when they're sexually dissatisfied, and when they feel like there's no hope of ever getting back the feelings they had when they were younger. You can be that girl again. You are her deep down. Release her and all of her energy.

· STEP 5 ·

Bond with Your Home

Bring back the art of homemaking

Start vacuuming

Play with your children

My easy morning routine

Be prepared!

Don't expect your husband to clean

Create a place of beauty

Plant some flowers and teach your children to appreciate nature

Really talk to your children

One of the most important contributions to your family, I think, is creating a beautiful environment for your children to grow up in. Isn't living in a place full of wonderful memories and traditions one of the best blessings of life? Gathering around the kitchen table, planting bulbs in autumn, marking your child's growth on the walls, being part of a community, creating roots, and filling your house with joy and laughter—this is what makes a happy family.

If you're not connected to your home, you'll have a hard time being a happy house-wife. Since this is the place you'll spend most of your time, you need to enjoy being there. I could stay in the house for days—I'm a hermit most of the time. I joke that weeks go by when I don't leave the kitchen. Sometimes it seems as if all I do is cook breakfast, clean up, cook lunch, clean up, cook dinner, clean up, then start all over again the next day.

Being in my kitchen gives me an enormous amount of joy. Cooking is my hobby, and every day I'm trying new recipes. Cleaning, however, I can pretty much do without. But I do want a clean house, so I have to do it. I've created a system, and now everything flows perfectly. My house looks gorgeous, and that makes me happy.

I think a lot of housewives become desperate as they try to juggle all the chores needed to keep their homes tidy and running smoothly. A lot of women I know complain that they just cannot stay on top of all the housework. But you do want your house to be neat and beautiful, right? It's important for your entire family. I don't want you to go crazy trying to keep your tile shiny, so follow my tips and see how much easier your day goes.

Hey, believe me, no one wants to spend the day mopping the floors. There's nothing I like less than knowing I have to fold and put away another load of laundry. I hate it. But no matter how much I hate it or put it off, it will still be there in the morning, and it will continue to pile up. So, I have a motto that I live by: If you think it, do it.

I'd love to have a reality show where cameras follow me all day and I show the girls how to pull off the housewife gig. I've figured out that if you don't put things off for to-morrow, if you have a schedule, and if you know that you just cannot do everything every day, well then, it all works in sync.

I admit that I'm a control freak. I like to wake up, make the beds, wipe down the bath-room counters, grab all the dirty clothes, put a load of laundry in, turn on the coffee pot, put on a little makeup, and throw on a cute pair of jeans and a T-shirt before I wake the kids up for school.

I love my house. I love my family. What is more fulfilling than taking care of my fam-ily and creating a beautiful home? Nothing. So, keeping my home neat and clean is a pri-ority in my life. I know if you stay on a schedule, it doesn't get out of control.

Bring Back the Art of Homemaking

Maybe you think that you have to make priorities in your life, and since you're so busy with the children, keeping your house clean is at the bottom of the list. I say that there's no excuse for a dirty, messy house. You can keep it clean, and you should. You can have it beautiful, and you should. Your home is a reflection on you, and if it's a dirty, filthy mess, then what does that say about you, your family, your children? Do you want your children to grow up in that? Do you want your kids to bring their friends home to that? No.

I've been to houses where every room is filled with toys. I have girlfriends who haven't seen the tops of their kitchen counters in years. Some women live with clutter. Some women live without any organization. Some women live without a schedule. Maybe it works for them, but I find that when everything has a place and you keep on top of it, little by little each day, then you never have to spend an entire day cleaning house. The way I do it, you straighten up and clean for about an hour in the morning and an hour at night, and you're off house duty for the rest of the day. The secret is that you cannot put anything on hold. If you forget it, you'll regret it.

I watched as my sister's new apartment quickly became smothered with clothes. The first time I went there, in the corner was a pile of clothes that needed to be folded and put away. The next time I went, the pile was double in size. I was there last night, and the clothes have taken over half of her living room. I went crazy—the sight of all these wrinkled clothes was too much for me to take. When I asked her why she hadn't put the clothes away, she said that they were all too wrinkled, and she'll get to it when she has time.

What a nightmare. If she had only folded the first batch and put it away, her clothes would be under control. Now they're chaos. Her excuse is that she's so busy being a mom, taking college courses, and working part time, and at the end of the day she's tired. I feel sorry for her, but she cannot use these excuses to let her life be out of control.

I've said this before, but I find it so aggravating when I hear women acting desperate and whining that they never seem to have enough time in the day to get everything done. Well, you know what? I get it all done, and you could too. With every luxury that is available today, the life of a housewife is a breeze. Who are you kidding with this out-of-control act? Enough!

When Connor was four months old, I invited about twenty people over for Christmas Eve—my family, some friends, and Bill's family. I cooked a gorgeous dinner from scratch, my house was clean, my baby was fed. My sister-in-law called to say she just couldn't come for dinner because she didn't have her act together, since tomorrow was Christmas and all. She still hadn't wrapped her presents.

She had two children, ages ten and nine, and a husband who got home every day at 5:00, yet the night before Christmas she was still trying to get it together. I thought it was funny because here I was with an infant, nursing every four hours, a husband who worked late every night, and yet I was able to pull a traditional homemade Christmas Eve dinner together for twenty people, and my gifts were all wrapped.

Now I know I'm more compulsive than a lot of women, but I just don't know why so many women use their position as mother as an excuse not to have it together. This attitude is really played out, I think. If you're a housewife, you have the whole day, every day, to do the chores and take care of the kids, and I know you can do it. If you follow my schedule and get organized, your home life will run so smoothly that you'll be able to do a lot of other things, like enjoying your home, your family, your life.

Start Vacuuming

It's possible to keep your house tidy without going crazy. Oh, I know that cleaning is not on our A list of things to do in life, but it's got to be done, so why whine about it? No matter how much you wish the sink full of dishes would disappear, it's not going to happen unless you put the gloves on and start scrubbing. Hey, it totally sucks to have to scrub the pots, I know—I hate it. But I put on my gloves and do it. In fact, I've found that if I just don't think about it and go ahead and do it, I feel much better. I've even started to challenge myself to see how quickly I can get everything tidied up in my house at the end of the day before my husband comes home. I have it down to fifteen minutes.

Does this sound crazy to you? Maybe. But for some reason—maybe it's because Bill and I used to work together, and deep inside I still am a little competitive with him, or maybe it's because I just refuse to let him think I can't handle it—I won't let him see the house out of control. I like for him to walk in the door to a clean, beautiful home. Right before he pulls into the driveway I do my quick pick-up. I throw all the toys into the basket, the dirty clothes into the hamper, and the dishes into the dishwasher, and I straighten out the house.

You may think this is a little extreme, but isn't it my job to keep our home clean, beautiful, and under control? Isn't the job of a housewife to care for the home?

What about the job of mother? If my children were hungry, dirty, and failing in school, wouldn't that make me a bad mother? Yes. We work hard to be great moms, so why would we want to fail our homes? Having a beautiful home is an important part of a child's life. You could be poor and still have a beautiful home. My grandparents didn't have any money to spend on luxuries for their home, but you know what? It was always clean, everything had its place, there was never clutter, and it always looked like a pretty little place that you'd want to visit for the day and drink some lemonade. My grandmother scrubbed her walls and her floors, and they sparkled. She had pride in her home—her two-bedroom home where she raised *nine children* who were always clean and well behaved.

My grandmother was raised in an era when keeping your home beautiful was a status symbol—something women were proud of.

This is not the case today.

I hear a lot of women say that doing housework is beneath them; they have better things to do than scrub the floor. I agree. Sometimes there are more important things to do than scrub the floor. So be smart and buy the Swiffer, and when your floor is really dirty, try my favorite trick: take two old washcloths, soak them in hot soapy water, wring them out, put them under your feet, and dance around the room. It cleans the floor and gets your legs in shape at the same time.

The trick is that you don't wash the floors every week, except maybe the kitchen, which gets a lot of traffic, so you might mop it every four days or so. Maybe you could stretch out the real nitty-gritty cleaning as long as your house looks tidy; this will save you some time. But the cleaning has to be done eventually. You want your babies to crawl on clean floors, don't you? I agree that you shouldn't spend every waking moment as a slave to your house, but having pride in your home and keeping it nice is very important to your family. You're selling your family short if you bail out and think that you cannot do it all, or worse yet, if you feel overwhelmed and give up.

So many women now actually refuse to do housework, or refuse to clean, like somehow it's someone else's job. Why is taking care of your home and family beneath you?

I hear many women brag about how they only make reservations for dinner, or they joke about not knowing where their kitchen is. Recently, I overheard a mother tell another mom that she hasn't cooked a meal in twenty years—that her children are trained to grab something to eat on their way home from school. I wanted to ask her what she thought they would grab that would be nutritious, or why she thought it wasn't important to eat dinner with her kids. I wondered what could possibly be more important than preparing a meal for her children, but I just kept my mouth shut. I'll get more into the cooking thing later, but first let me finish telling you about this conversation.

The other woman responded that she, too, hates to be in the kitchen. She said, "What, do I have nothing better to do than cook and clean all day? I'd feel like a servant—that's why they have immigrants."

I was outraged. It took all my might not to say something to these two princesses. I looked over at them. They didn't look like royalty. In fact, they looked like the rest of us, except that for some reason they have come up with the notion that they're too good for housekeeping. I'm sad for them. They're missing out on a real blessing in their life—bonding with their home.

Being in an environment you love, building a nest for your little chickadees, playing house, and taking care of hubby is a lot of fun. These women are empty. I wonder if they really don't enjoy taking care of their homes, or if they just have to put on this act to be cool.

I've noticed that there's definitely peer pressure lately not to clean, not to cook, not to care about the home. Life is apparently supposed to center on working out, going to the salon, and doing God knows what, and for some reason women are ashamed to say they're keeping house, or—oh my goodness, can I say it?—*liking* it.

Why do women today feel embarrassed to say they cooked a meal, baked a cake, planted a rosebush, or scrubbed a toilet? When did it become someone else's job to take care of your home?

I can empathize with these women somewhat. As you know, for a while I got caught up in the whole desperate housewife syndrome. For six months I, too, had a full-time cleaning woman/nanny. Thank God I realized I was turning into a blob and snapped out of it!

I'm so happy I got over myself and learned how to bond with my home. I'm happy every day to be here, making it the best place for my family. I told you how I love when it rains really hard or snows so much that the children and I are trapped in the house. It's as if I'm being forced to stay in, and those are the really great moments. If you think about it, I bet you like that, too—nature giving you the freedom to stay home. No errands, no expectations, just you and the kids stuck at home all day.

I hope you really enjoy those days bonding with your home and your children. Like Martha Stewart says, it's a good thing.

Just thinking of Martha, my idol, makes me happy. Here's a woman who really enjoys vacuuming. She has made a billion-dollar empire out of homemaking. She's wearing cute clothes, gardening, brushing the dogs, and whipping up a butternut squash soup while most women are complaining about how hard they have it. She has taught the world that indeed there's an art to homemaking. Martha is right. Creating a beautiful home filled with joy and laughter, the smell of apple pie, with dogs and kids running amok . . . isn't that what we all strive for? Family, friends, home, and love is what life is all about.

Oh, I know what you're probably thinking, Martha Stewart has a staff of people helping her pull it off—no one could be that perfect. Well, I agree. I make priorities. I definitely don't have time to brush my dog every day, so I do it only once a week. I have quite a few junk drawers, and I don't fold underwear. I have a lot of shortcuts, and I realize that I'm not going to be able to get everything done that I expect, so I let myself off the hook a lot. The key here is to not put too much on my to-do list. I pick a couple of chores to do each day, an errand or two, I make sure I keep time for myself, playtime with my children, and time for my husband. Here's how I do it.

My Schedule

Every Day

- Make the bed as soon as you wake up.
- Wash up—do your makeup, throw on some jeans and a T-shirt—cute and tight, of course.

- Wipe down the bathroom counter when you leave the bathroom in the morning. Wipe mirrors; my kids always spit toothpaste onto them. I keep Windex wipes under the sink.
- Do a load of laundry every morning, fold it, and put it away as soon as it's dry. If you leave the clothes in the dryer, they'll wrinkle and you'll have to iron.
- Get the kids off to school and immediately straighten up the kitchen.
- Sit for a few minutes and meditate, pray, stretch.
- Do that day's chores: vacuuming, cleaning bathrooms, dusting.
- When the kids come home from school, collect their hats, coats, and shoes and put them away. After first grade, start asking them to do it themselves.
- Make dinner as the children do their homework. Clean up as you go. I never sit down to eat with a mess in the kitchen.
- Playtime.
- Get the children ready for bed.
- Relaxation time for mommy.

Every Week

- *Monday and Friday:* Vacuum.
- *Tuesday:* Clean the bathrooms.
- *Wednesday:* Change and wash the sheets (yes, I do this only once a week unless a child throws up on the bed or there's some other disaster. Ladies, let yourselves off the hook—I don't know any woman who changes her sheets more than that, so don't worry).
- *Thursday:* Dust (use a damp cloth; it collects the particles instead of just moving them around).
- *Friday:* Shop for groceries.
- *Saturday and Sunday:* I do a quick straightening out in the morning, fluffing pillows, maybe a load of laundry, and that's it. I spend my week-

end with my husband and my children having fun, being outside, having some time to myself while Bill watches the children, and cooking big dinners. I don't spend my weekends cleaning. We often have company on the weekends, and often I entertain and spend a lot of time in the kitchen.

The key point here is that I give myself the weekend off. Just like my husband, I'm not working, and since I don't love cleaning chores, I wait until Monday to go back to work. I think this is a great system, and it feels good to know you have the weekend off. When you don't have any expectations of yourself, it's very relaxing. Give yourself a day or two off. During that time when you have your husband at home, take a nap, go for a walk, read a book, go shopping, take the children to a movie, get a sitter and go out with your husband to dinner, and enjoy yourself.

Once a Week

- Mop the floors (mop the kitchen floor every few days or as needed).

Once a Month

- Clean inside the refrigerator.
- Straighten out the drawers and closets.
- Vacuum the drapes and wipe down the blinds.

Seasonal

- Every few months, wash the windows.
- Vacuum the ceilings and dust the chandeliers.

- Deep-clean the floor and carpets (I use a steam cleaner).
- Wipe down the walls. My children get fingerprints on everything, so when you paint be sure you tell the man at the hardware store that you have children and you want washable paint.
- Wipe down your kitchen cabinetry. Clean first with a damp cloth with a little wood cleaner, then use some lemon oil to make them shine.
- Each spring, give your house a complete overhaul. Take a couple of weeks and clean the entire house thoroughly from top to bottom—even changing your air conditioning filters. Martha Stewart has a great spring cleaning guide that you could find on the Internet, and, of course, there are many books available that take you through this process step by step.
- Each fall, get your chimneys swept.
- Have a licensed technician make sure your burner is clean and working for the upcoming winter.
- Check all the batteries in the smoke detectors.
- Clean your radiators before the heat comes on.

Remember, I like to do these chores in the morning and get them out of the way. I set a goal for myself to have everything done by noon so I have some time for errands and for myself in the afternoon. Plus, I try not to clean later in the day when the children are at home. I make sure I have free time to play with them.

Make sure you save time to play with your children. Schedule that, too.

Play with Your Children

This should be pretty obvious, but last night I was watching ABC's *Supernanny*, and the nanny, Jo Frost, actually had to tell a dad to play with his four children. He was at home with them all day but never thought of playing with them or taking them out in the yard. Frost got this father to take the children out on the swing set, and when the mom came home she was gleaming with joy to see them having fun. I was shocked. I just cannot believe parents out there are not playing or interacting with their children. It's crucial to get on the floor and play with your toddler. Spending that one-on-one time is important not only for the child but also for the parent. I know it's exhausting. My back sometimes feels as if it could break as I sit on the floor building blocks. My tushy gets numb. Of course I don't love every minute of it. Like all moms, I try to secretly do other things while the kids think I'm playing. *Star* magazine is usually set up just next to the dollhouse. As they grow older they still yearn to play with you. Connor and I now play checkers and Trouble.

Every day you must take time to play with your children. Push them on a swing, play a game, tickle them on the floor. Last night I broke three nails playing basketball with Connor in the driveway at 8:00 in the dark. Did I have to do this? No, but for the fifteen minutes I was out there we had a lot of laughs, I wore him out a bit, and when I tucked him into bed, he said, "Mom, you're really cool." Memories like that will stay with both of us forever.

Don't get me wrong. Sometimes mommy just doesn't have time to play. I know we have chores to do. This morning Hannah wanted to play dolls with me. I didn't want to. I wanted to just lounge around and drink my coffee. As I was sitting in the kitchen reading the newspaper and watching *The Tony Danza Show*, I could hear her calling my name over and over, "Mommy, please . . . Mommy, please . . . just for a few minutes." The poor thing. I got up, brought my coffee, sat with her, and played house.

You have to set aside time each day to play with your children one on one. Get outside and play a game of tag. Go in your family room and play Twister. Play hide and seek. Laugh together. Have fun together.

You could also get your children on board with cleaning duty. It's important for children to have chores and to earn their own money. Connor and Hannah both have to straighten up their rooms each morning. Hannah is in charge of making sure Paddy, our dog, has clean water, and Connor has to walk her each afternoon. They both get an allowance of five dollars each week. I also ask them to help me clean. They love to wash windows because, of course, they love to use the spray bottle.

Some Tips to Make Your Life Easier

1. *Write down everything you need. You could pop your head trying to remember all the information you have to hold onto. School events, birthday parties, Little League games, play dates—when you book something, write it down. I keep a Palm Pilot with me, and as soon as I book something I jot it down in the calendar.*

2. *Keep Post-it pads in every room, along with a sharpened pencil, especially in the kitchen and next to your bed. When you think of something you need to get or do, make a note. Stick it on your forehead if you have to.*

3. *Make a playroom. Buy some baskets, fill them with toys in one room, and don't let toys take over the house.*

4. *Keep the dining room and living room off limits to kids.*

5. *If you keep your house straightened up, it will always look clean.*

6. *Get rid of the clutter. Throw half of your stuff away—you don't need it.*

7. *Get everything off your kitchen counters.*

8. *Don't buy in bulk—where are you going to store it all?*

9. *Make sure your children eat all messy foods in the kitchen only.*

10. *If they stain their clothing, remove it immediately to soak.*

11. *Keep toilet cleaner, paper towels, glass cleaner, extra toilet paper, and tissues in each bathroom.*

12. *Every few days do a quick wash of the toilet. I like Ajax.*

13. *Spray and wipe the shower down before you get out. Keep clean shower spray right there in the tub/shower area.*

14. *Wipe the bath down as soon as you get out, while it's still wet, to keep the bath ring away.*

15. *Either hang your clothes back up or put them in the hamper as soon as you take them off.*

16. *I always wear my jeans two or three times before I wash them. I also use the same towel a few times to save on laundry time.*

17. *After you use something, put it back where it came from.*

18. *Organize, organize, organize!*

My Easy Morning Routine

Here's how I pull all this together in a regular day.

I shower every other morning. I think showering every day is bad for your skin and hair. In the winter I even go every three days. My Italian grandmother and her sisters all had beautiful skin. The secret is not to overwash.

The same goes for my children. Unless it's summer and they're sweaty or have chlorine or sunscreen on them and need a bath, I bathe them every three days. Think of your skin like tissue paper; it's very delicate. You can see on the faces of women who worship the sun, or go to the tanning salon, or—even worse—don't use moisturizer, and they look all dried-up and wrinkly. The natural oils of your skin are very healthy for you. If you have acne or bad skin, overwashing it isn't the answer. Changing your diet is the best thing you can do to keep your skin clear. Another great thing you could do is to buy some dazzling diamond earrings; not only will you feel great, but everyone will be staring at your ears and not the crow's-feet around your eyes.

I'm not one to apply a full face of makeup unless I'm going out at night. During the day I never wear foundation, although I think I should probably start, but I just don't have time and can't be bothered. I rinse my face in the morning and apply moisturizer. And I always wear eye shadow (I prefer a brown shade), mascara, and *always* lipstick. I brush my hair, and I'm ready.

If you keep your closet organized, and if you only keep things in there that you'll actually wear, getting dressed each day is a snap. I have about twenty versions of the same T-shirt that I love in long and short sleeves, and eight pairs of the same jeans with slight variations. If you're consumed with what you wear, you'll waste too much time in the morning. I used to spend about three minutes trying to find matching socks, and then I finally went out and bought thirty pairs of socks and one of those sock drawer organizers from the Lillian Vernon catalog, and now I have my socks right there for me. Get organized. It makes your life easier.

Also, I always buy in outfits. Last week I bought some cute lime green linen Capri pants, and right then I made sure I grabbed a matching shirt and sandals.

The biggest point here is the less you have to think each morning, the quicker you'll get ready and out the door.

Choose what your children will wear to school the night before; after you tuck them in, pull out an outfit and hang it over their footboard. When they wake up they'll see it there and put it on.

The night before, make sure you put any lunch money, snacks, vitamins, notes, or homework that you'll need in the morning on the kitchen island or in a spot where you'll see these items and not forget them. No matter how organized I think I am, and no matter how much I prepare, it seems as if something always goes wrong in the morning and I forget something.

The problem is that my kids just won't move as fast as I need them to. I think we all have this problem. For this I have no answer except to suggest that you don't lose your temper in the process. Getting upset in the morning will only make the children upset, and then you all start the day in a bad mood. Instead, laugh it off and don't let anything bother you. When Connor refuses to get out of bed and I start to feel my blood boil, I just walk away for a minute, take a breath, and come back and try again.

Some days the children are just miserable. I can be a pushover, I admit it. They're so young, and will be for such a short time. So, once in a while I let the children lounge around. Connor is a perfect student, getting all good grades, so a couple of times this winter I woke him up only to tell him I was going to let him stay home with me. This is such a thrill for a little seven-year-old, and really, who cares? He's in second grade, and he has at least fourteen more years of school ahead of him. Hannah missed school the other day because she wanted to lie on the couch and watch *Shrek*. I let her. So what? I think it's the days like that, being with mommy on the couch watching a movie with a big bowl of popcorn that we just popped together, that are important. In fact, this Friday I'm going to let Connor play hooky, and we're going to see the dinosaurs at the American Museum of Natural History in New York City.

Anyway, back to the point I was trying to make. Each morning, judge what is happening in your house with your family. Don't kill yourself trying to be perfect. Don't torture your children trying to make them perfect either. I've sent Connor off to school without brushing his hair. I've sent him off without brushing his teeth. I've let Hannah go to school with mismatched socks. I've forgotten to give them lunch money. I've forgotten to pack snacks.

I can remember when I was a child, my mother embarrassed me every day at the bus stop trying to force oatmeal down my throat. I swore I would never do this to my children, and guess what? I chased after Connor today and was spoon-feeding him his Cheerios at the bus stop, and he got really mad at me.

The bottom line is to try to make your mornings easy.

I try to get up an hour before my kids. Jump in the shower (or not) and do my makeup and hair. I make the bed and straighten out the bathroom. I throw on jeans and a T-shirt. I throw a load of laundry in and put on a pot of coffee.

Then I wake up the kids. While they brush their teeth I make the beds. I get them dressed and bring them down and make breakfast. You can give them cereal or toast, but add an apple or banana. Try to make scrambled eggs, French toast, or pancakes a couple of days a week. Yogurt drinks are always good to have on hand for mornings when you're rushing out the door. If they only get to eat a little bit, I make them drink a yogurt on their way to the bus stop. While they're eating I quickly straighten up the kitchen. I, of course, drink a few cups of coffee each morning. You can have all this going on at once and get the kids to the bus stop on time, coffee in hand.

When I get back from the bus stop I still have Hannah with me, since she doesn't go to preschool until noon. I put on a television show for her, set her up with paint or clay in the kitchen, or give her a few dolls, and I go around the house in my mad rush to get it under control. I collect all the dirty clothes from the hampers and put on a load of laundry. I vacuum the kitchen and empty the garbage pails.

Before I begin my daily cleaning regimen, I take a few minutes to breathe deeply, stretch, and meditate. This is a great treat you need to do for yourself every morning.

Then I get moving. As you know, each day I focus on a different chore. Tuesdays I clean all the bathrooms. On a different day I change the sheets. A different day I mop. If you keep everything in order and do things day by day, your house won't look dirty.

By the time I'm done straightening up the house, Hannah is more awake and ready to play. I get down on the floor and play with Barbies, play hide and seek, whatever she wants.

Whatever toys we take out, we put back into the bins when we're done. This is important, because you know how easy it is for toys to take over the entire house. I have friends who have toys in their living room, dining room, everywhere. Don't do this. Keep all the toys in one room, preferably not one near the entry hall. Pick a room that has a door and put a few baskets in with covers on them for the toys. If the playroom does get out of control, you can always shut the door.

Then it's time to do something for yourself. Even when Hannah was a toddler I joined a gym and took her with me three mornings a week. Most gyms have child care. I don't recommend this for a baby, but a two-year-old can safely sit and play blocks for an hour while mommy has a workout.

If you do have a baby, there are a lot of exercises you can do at home. I lost my baby weight with Jane Fonda's aerobic tapes right in my living room.

On days you don't go to the gym, go shopping with a girlfriend, bring your tots, and have lunch out. Bonding with other at-home moms is really crucial to staying happy at home with your kids. You need someone in your situation to hang out with, and it's great for your little one to have a playmate.

In the afternoon, go to the grocery store and run your errands.

Make sure you set time aside each day to have some relaxation. Hannah is now in pre-school, but before that she napped for a couple of hours. If you have your child at home with you, you could put him in the playpen with some toys, put the swing in front of *Sesame Street*, or let him play next to you on the floor. Just make sure that you have set aside some time for you to sit back, flip through a magazine, have a cup of tea, and get rejuvenated.

Some days are hectic, I know. Some days I run errands and have no time for any relaxation. On very busy days I make sure that I take it easy on myself later in the day. At some point during the day, you should take at least one half hour for yourself, even if it's at 9:00 in the evening.

My son gets off the bus at 4:00, and by then I have picked out what I'm making for dinner. While he does his homework at my kitchen island, I prepare dinner. You can make great homemade dinners in thirty minutes every day.

I clean up after dinner and then the kids and I have playtime.

Then before getting the kids ready for bed, here's an important thing: We go around and pick up all the toys off the floor. Then I get everything organized, and it really takes only about ten minutes to do the whole house. If you put this stuff off, it will just fester in your mind.

Most women have their husbands come home at a decent hour to help. If this is the case, then you really have nothing to complain about. My husband usually doesn't come home until 8:00 or 9:00, so I bathe the kids and get them into bed.

Like most mothers, I look forward to my late night hours when I'm off duty. It's then that we get to cuddle up with a good book, watch a trashy movie, or have some time to spend with our husbands. If you follow my schedule, you'll find yourself less stressed, and at the end of the day you'll actually feel relaxed and in control of your life and your family.

Be Prepared!

Part of having a smooth-running household is having things in place *before* you have an emergency and desperately need them.

In the kitchen. Make sure you have meat, milk, and bread in your freezer. You can buy these items fresh and freeze them for up to two months. It really is a nightmare to dress the children and have to run out to get milk when it's cold outside.

Always have hors d'oeuvres in your freezer in case you have last-minute company. There are so many great things on the market today. I love the spinach dip and Southwestern egg rolls from TGIF. Also, you can buy frozen guacamole, pigs in blankets, and my absolute favorite, potato pancakes. So keep some jarred salsa and bags of tortillas in your pantry, and you're set in case some friends stop in. For the children, you must have frozen pizza.

In the bathroom. Check your medicine cabinets every six months for outdated meds. Make sure you always have the following on hand for your children:

Children's Tylenol
Children's Motrin
Children's Benadryl
Children's Pedialyte
Thermometer
Neosporin
Bandages
And for Mom—Tylenol and earplugs are essential!

For emergency gifts. Keep a stash of wrapping paper, a variety of cards, and a few presents in a closet. I have been stuck a few times when I bumped into a girlfriend who said it was her birthday, so I always have backup gifts in the house—a bottle of perfume, candles, a scarf, and a piece of fun costume jewelry in a drawer. My children are always invited to last-minute parties and I hate having to run out for a gift, so I always have a few toys that would be good for a girl or boy. And in case you get a last-minute dinner invitation, be sure you have a few bottles of good wine or some type of hostess gift in your stash to bring with you.

Don't Expect Your Husband to Clean

If you wait around for your husband to come home and start mopping the floor, you'll really become desperate. Give it up already. I told you to stop nagging your husband. You've just got to stop expecting him to do his share around the house. It isn't going to happen. It's your job anyway, so just do it.

Yes, I'm letting him off the hook. If you expect your husband to do as much as you do around the house, if you expect him to clean the way you do, if you expect him to care about the house the way you do, you'll end up deeply resentful.

I'm so excited that my husband makes the bed on the weekends. I'm so excited when he vacuums the kitchen floor. I get so excited when he does a load of laundry that for me it's foreplay. The reason I get so excited when he does anything around the house is that it's icing on the cake for me, because I think the household chores fall under my jurisdiction. Yes, ladies, it's true: If you're home full time, it's part of your job to take care of the house.

I can hear the screaming now. Calm down and listen to me for a minute. I'm so sick of hearing women whine that their husbands don't help around the house. Well, I already told you that if you start turning up the heat in the bedroom you'll see a newly domestic side to your man, but put that aside for a minute. If he's working all day at a full-time job, forty or fifty hours a week or more, not to mention the commuting time, do you really think it's fair (Hold on, Connor is flipping out, I need to help him with some kids' site on the computer. . . . Okay, I'm back) for you to expect your husband to clean at the end of the day?

Don't get me wrong. I know men who leave their underwear on the floor, their snot rags on the bedside table, and their dirty dishes on the table. This is not acceptable, and I wouldn't tolerate it. Your husband cannot be allowed to be a complete slob or to abuse his role in the house. From the first day of marriage, you have to talk to your husband and tell him what you expect of him—that he has to pull his own weight around the house and not contribute to the mess. But other than that, I think you should get off his back.

I have friends who have spent years saying the same things to their husbands, and by now I'm sick of hearing it. My mother has been complaining for forty years that my father is a slob. Well, it's too late now, I tell her. She should have trained him when they first got married. Now she just needs to shut up and wipe down the bathroom sink when he's done shaving. Yes, he's a slob, I agree. But he spent his life installing central air conditioners and breathed in so many chemicals that now he has some skin ailment. They live comfortably because of all his hard work, while my mother was able to stay home with her girls, which was her dream. So, look at the big picture, wipe down the freaking counter, and shut up. When my father does clean a pan, she's the first one to tell him what a bad job he did. "Look at this pot," she'll say to him, "Does this look clean to you?"

It's no wonder a lot of men back off from doing things around the house—they feel as if they just cannot do anything right. Bill used to get upset with me because I never let him just do things his way. I would put my two cents in on every little thing, until one day he blew up at me. We had a long talk about it, and I've learned to back off. He bathes the children differently. He makes them stand up to rinse them off with the shower hose. This drives me crazy, but I have learned to zip it. When he thinks he's helping me by vacuuming the kitchen floor after dinner when the children have dropped a million crumbs, I cringe as I hear him bang the vacuum into my furniture, nicking up my wood, but I zip it. Yes, he loads the dishwasher wrong every single time, and just yesterday morning, after living in this house for two years, he said, "So, how do you use the oven?"

He never wipes his feet. I cannot get him to take off his shoes when he comes in at night, and I am completely freaked out that he's tracking in New York City scum onto the very floors where my children play, and I cannot—though I have been trying for ten years—even get him to bring down his wet towel in the morning after he showers. So you know what? I carry it down in the morning. Big deal.

This is my house. Yes, ladies, we do have that. These are our houses. Even though our hubbies are paying for them, we know deep down that they're really ours. We've created these homes, and we know if our husbands ever walk out on us that we're going to stay planted in them while they continue to pay the mortgage. We know we really are the ones who run the household. We know we're the ones who make a house a home. It's the woman in charge of the house. Remember Ralph Kramden calling himself king of the castle? If you watched *The Honeymooners*, you knew it was his wife, Alice, who really ran things at home. She was in charge. Women, we're all in charge.

I always joke that we have all the power, because girls, we do have all the sexual power. As long as your husband wants it from you, you can get him to do anything you want. Just stop nagging him about it. Believe me, if you back off, start looking better, stop whining, start putting out, and stop expecting your husband to be you, everything will turn around. But don't expect miracles.

I know there are the husbands out there like Colin, my friend Dana's husband, who mops the floor, cleans the windows, and cooks dinner, but he's at home full time. I know there are men out there who are neat freaks, and to me that would be worse. I have a friend whose husband freaks out if she doesn't keep the house perfectly clean. He cleans the kitchen after she does and criticizes how she cleans. This is a disaster. So yes, let my husband be at work all day—I can handle it all. Let him help out when he wants to. Let him freeze his ass off on the train while I sleep until 9:00. Let him leave his towel on the floor. Who cares? In the grand scheme of things it really doesn't matter. What matters is that I'm married to a good man who has given me beautiful children and a beautiful home.

Create a Place of Beauty

Let's say you're organized, you're on a schedule, and you know how to get your home in order. How about taking the next step and making it beautiful? A little decorating magic and you'll start loving your house even more. Loving how your home looks and being happy to walk into it will make you very happy.

Let's face it, we all want to live in showcase homes, and while that might be a bit out of reach for most of us, it's not that hard to turn our ranches and colonials into our own private sanctuaries. The fact is, coming home at the end of the day to a place where you, your husband, and your children want to cuddle up on the couch with a good movie, a home that inspires your children to invite their friends, a home that's an inviting place for friends and family to gather together—that's what we all want. We all want our homes to be warm, cozy, and comfy, right? We all want the American dream of having the pretty yellow house with the white picket fence. No matter what your house looks like, no matter how big or small it is, as long as you have your family living there with you and as long as you have love, it will be your home. Let's turn your house into the home of your dreams. I'm going to show you that a little housewife elbow grease can go a long way. So, roll up your sleeves and let's get started.

I recently decided to wallpaper the bathroom in my master bedroom. I bought a gorgeous monkey print from a wallpaper website, and it looks great on the walls. My bathroom has the jungle safari theme I was looking for. Unfortunately, I ran out of wallpaper, and if you look closely at one wall, you can see the seam in the spot that I patched and the monkey's tail is chopped in half. So, I learned not to cheap out and always buy an extra double roll. For twenty-four dollars in savings I ruined my bathroom. When I have the energy, I'll pull the paper down and rehang it. I just reordered the same wallpaper, with an extra roll.

When I ordered the monkey print, my friend Gina said she loved it but would have been afraid to put it up. She asked how I came up with the idea. Well, I copied a bathroom I saw in a model home.

Yes, I am a home crasher. Whenever there's a model home or an open house, I stop in. I love to see how they're decorated. Whatever I like, I copy. The funny thing is, a lot of my girlfriends are copying me now. They love the way my house looks and ask me for decorating advice for their homes.

Mostly, I have no idea what to do. Decorating is such a difficult thing. The best thing to do is to copy other homes. Look through magazines, check out the displays in the furniture stores, and explore online. I am obsessed with the website realtor.com, where you can go on virtual tours of homes all over the country. You can tour million-dollar homes and get decorating ideas. It's fun.

One thing I do know is that color can turn the coldest house into the warmest home. When we moved into this house, every wall was white. It was so cold and uninteresting.

The first thing I did was paint all the rooms my favorite colors: creamy yellow, celery green, and cranberry red on the walls, with white trim. It warmed up the house immediately.

I read in a home decorating manual that you need to start out with a color scheme and a furniture style to carry through the house. This became my color scheme for the house, and I worked with those three colors when I shopped for furniture and rugs. I decided I liked country French furniture the best, so that was the style I chose (mixed with a touch of Southern charm, because I love the South and wish I was living in Charleston instead of Long Island, but that's another fact of my life that I cannot change right now, so I try not to think about it!). I think I have pulled it off a little bit—Southern charm with a French twist—and my house is starting to look good. I need to do a lot more, and just like you I have to prioritize one project at a time, so I'm trying to decide what to do next—buy more furniture for the living room or put granite on my kitchen counters. I have a budget, just like you, and have to decide what will make me happier. I think the granite . . . or maybe the furniture. I cannot decide.

This is our fourth house since we've been married. We started with a small home, and I have been riding the real estate wave for ten years, moving up every three years or so. My son is getting too old for this, and I have to make some roots, so we'll see if we stay in this house awhile. Anyway, I have changed my decorating style with each house. I started out with ultramodern taste. My dishes, glasses, couches, and dining table were black. Yuck! Then I was into the whole Southwest thing—remember the early 1990s, when everything had a cactus on it? Then I moved on to the beach motif, and my tables were rotted wood with overstuffed white couches—definitely not good for kids, I learned. After spending years restyling, redecorating, and mostly wasting a whole lot of money, I learned one thing: not to go with what is in style at the moment.

I should have listened to my mother. When I first got married and was out picking all of my ultramodern junk, my mother said to go traditional. She was right. Now I'm more traditional, and I buy classic furniture that will stay in style.

So, my advice is to look through the design books, ask your family and friends, and speak to a decorator. Furniture stores usually give decorating service for free. Then, before you buy anything, really sit with the idea for a few days. Through the years I have wasted so much money on stuff that I bought because it was on sale or I just acted in the spur of the moment. Don't get caught up in getting everything done in a minute. Take your time. My house is still not decorated completely. I'm looking around and waiting for just the right pieces.

You don't need a lot of money to make your house beautiful. A gallon of fresh paint, a slipcover, and some flowers can transform a room. If you don't have money for art, what is better art than photos of your family? Buy some pretty, basic frames and display the precious photos of your cutie pies. Look through your mother's attic and go to garage sales, tag sales, and estate sales. I've gotten a lot of great oldies from these backyard busters. In fact, the big old white rocking chair in my daughter's room with about thirty-five stuffed bunnies sitting on it cost me ten dollars at a tag sale last summer.

And don't forget that eclectic is in. You can mix and match furniture, upholstery, stripes and checks, flowers and prints, dark and light—it can all work together. You can buy different pieces of china, mix them together on the dining room table with some pretty napkins, and see how nice it looks.

Rearrange your furniture. Move the sofa. Refresh the room. Get rid of your junk. Invest in one nice thing to start with, maybe an armoire for your television set. Start looking at the home magazines. I love *Country Living* and *Southern Living*. Choose your style. Start making your house a home. Start making it pretty. You'll feel wonderful being in such a beautiful space. Your children will be proud to come home.

Plant Some Flowers and Teach Your Children to Appreciate Nature

What could help you bond with your home more than gardening? Getting outside with your children, your husband, a few shovels, and some seeds on a nice day—that's heaven. What on earth could be more peaceful than this? Tell me.

Just like Martha Stewart, I cannot wait for spring each year. What is more therapeutic than getting your hands in the dirt? Each year, my children and I plant about four hundred annual flowers in the garden come the first weekend in May. We have to wait until the last frost, and for me it's worse than being on a diet. Once we can finally get out there and start digging, the whole family enjoys this time together. The children love playing in the dirt, and they love awaiting the bloom of their little babies. They look out the window each day with anticipation of the first bud. This is a bonding process that I encourage all moms to do with their children. If you're not teaching your children about the wonders of this amazing land God gave us, I say shame on you. How will they ever appreciate nature if you don't teach them? I see cars going by me with children throwing their trash out the window. It makes me crazy to see that trash on the side of the highway. We all need to teach our children to love this earth. We need to teach them that they need to keep it clean.

This goes back to my problem with the selfish, desperate housewives of today. I think a lot of women are too afraid of ruining their manicures to go out and plant bulbs with their children. I doubt that many of these princess moms are pushing a wheelbarrow across their lawns. The landscaper will do it. It's too bad. How will your children learn the beauty of the garden without you? Think back to when you were a child. My mother used to lock us out the whole day in the spring and summer, and we had to play outside. We climbed tries, made mud pies, dug for worms, searched for caterpillars, jumped from our swings, sold lemonade at the corner, and chased fireflies at dusk.

Sending your child off to sleep-away camp all summer, driving from one activity to the next, setting up play dates—our children today are scheduled not for their enjoyment but for our avoidment (I made up that word, but it works here, don't you think?). A lot of children are booked to the max so their parents can avoid having to spend time with them. I have heard a thousand times from moms I know that they have to find something for Ben to do or he'll be jumping off the walls. How about this—let him outside! Let him run wild. Let him jump off the walls. Let him be a child. Give him some space. Children were meant to act their age. Let your seven-year-old son jump around like a moron. He doesn't need Ritalin, he doesn't have ADHD, he's just a boy with pent-up energy.

I know I'm getting off the whole gardening thing, but I'm coming back to it. And here it is. Let your children enjoy this earth. Bring them to the park. Let them chase butterflies. Let them roll around on the grass. Oh, and please don't drench your lawn with cancer-causing pesticides. They don't keep your grass greener, water does. Don't spray your trees with pesticides. It doesn't keep the bugs away, it only gets into your children's lungs. When it rains, all those chemicals get washed away, and you're not killing the bugs. In fact, if you let nature do her job, the good bugs would eat the bad bugs. You might as well wash your money down the drain. Plus, do you want all these chemicals on your lawn? Your children roll around, play, and run barefoot in the grass, not to mention the dog. I've never sprayed any of my properties, and I don't have any more bugs than my spraying neighbors. Check out the PBS gardener Jerry Baker for all the tips you need to have a great lawn. He's fabulous.

Please get outside with your children. Teach them not to pollute. Show them by example. Plant a tree and watch it grow with them. It will still be there for them to show their children. Decorate your bushes with cotton for Halloween, hang lights for Christmas, hide eggs in the lawn for Easter, and teach your children to appreciate the earth and all the wonders that come from it.

Planting flowers is such a marvelous thing, and it's a gift that keeps on giving. Pulling up to a house with bountiful blooms of flowers each season makes the home such a place of beauty. Have you ever seen a house with no flowers, nothing blooming? It's so depressing, so cold, so lifeless. Landscapes can bring so much enjoyment to your family. Hang a tire from a tree. Help your children make stepping-stones to place in your garden. Put a bench out in your yard and sit there and read a book with a cup of tea on a spring afternoon. How about a glass of lemonade garnished with some mint that you grew yourself in your very own garden?

I really envy the true green thumbed people out there. My grandfather recently won an award for growing the largest tomato in his town. Here is a man who spent his life out in his garden pulling figs, peaches, and berries from trees and creating delicious meals for his family. The devotion it takes to grow a healthy strawberry plant or a thriving patch of cucumbers is enormous. Each year, my husband and I plant several batches of fruits and vegetables in our garden.

I love going out into my yard to pick fresh parsley, basil, and tomatoes, and I just planted rosemary. I can't wait to stir it all together and create a nutritious, healthy salad for my family. It makes me feel great. I encourage all of you to start planting. It's really a rewarding experience.

Yes, it's also a lot of work. I'm not suggesting that you have to get out there and mow your own lawn unless you enjoy it, which my sister Cheryl loves. I think she mows her lawn every two days. And while she refuses to put her laundry away, she'll be outside weeding her flower beds, which is her favorite pastime. This is not a pleasure that I share.

I would much rather plant the flowers. I admit that I have never mowed a lawn, and I never will. I love to water my roses, but I dread dragging the hose across the lawn. But with every hobby, it takes dedication and pride to get results. A beautiful garden, with an abundance of color to cheer up your house, is really worth the effort, I think.

Bonding with nature, smelling the fresh air, watching your children blow the dandelions into the wind to make a wish . . . teaching them to appreciate nature is a gift they'll pass on to their children. Talk to your children about the wonders of nature. Talk to them about responsibility. . . . In fact, just talk to them.

Really Talk to Your Children

The other day Connor and I were outside planting geraniums. While we were there, just us and nature, I decided it was a good opportunity to talk to him about drugs. I know he's only seven, but I was reading on the Internet about a third-grade girl who was taking steroids. The article said that if you wait to talk to your kids about drugs until they're in the ninth grade, you're going to be way too late. So I said, "Connor, do you know what steroids are?"

Do you know what he said? "Yes, Mom, they're drugs that you drink." We went on talking about drugs. I told him about pills, needles, alcohol, cigarettes, and how he should never accept anything to eat from anyone but his very best friends, and that he should never do something he doesn't want to do. I know most moms out there are like me and think they're on top of this, but I'm worried sick that Connor might try drugs, and I just want to keep the lines of communication open. I'm going to be on top of everything that he does. I'm going to be watching, smelling, listening to everything both of my children do.

This is another reason that I doubt I'll ever go back to work full time. I just don't want them to be at home alone while I'm at work. When parents lose control over their children, they really become desperate. I have a friend whose teenage son is battling a drug habit. He's now at one of those boot camps, and his mother is beside herself. She doesn't know what to do. She said to me one day, "I wish I could turn back the clock. There are so many things I would do differently. I blame myself for this."

"Why?" I asked her.

"Because I was too afraid to talk to him about drugs or sex, because I didn't want him to know about it. I guess I was just in denial." By the way, her son is fifteen. So I urge all moms to keep the lines of communication open. Spend some time together. Spend time talking. Take your children outside and lounge around on the hammock tonight, gaze at the stars, and see what they tell you. Allow them to open up to you.

I believe if you bond with your home, if you help your children appreciate nature, if you play with them, talk to them, it is all connected in the grand scheme of life, and the beauty of it all will simply fall into place. Your family will be stronger. Your children will live fuller lives and you will be happier.

Take your children fishing. Have your children bury your husband in sand at the beach. Watch the glow in your daughter's eyes as she catches her first butterfly. Help your son collect praying mantis eggs and watch them hatch together. Let your children go out into your garden and make bouquets for you, even if it's ragweed that they choose.

Take pride in caring for your home, your yard, your community, and this entire planet. Get outside, feel the ground, look at the sky, teach your babies to appreciate this earth, and thank God for it all. Run through the grass with your family, smell the air right after a storm, build a snowman, let them make real snowcones, let them drink the rain, show them the sense of adventure that's inside you. I know you still have it, somewhere deep down.

· STEP 6 ·

Get Back in the Kitchen

Cook for your family

Talk at the table

Begin new traditions

Have fun!

Basic cooking

Recipes

I really cannot understand why women refuse to cook. For goodness' sake, it's time to cook your kid a decent meal. All the preservatives and artificial ingredients in fast food and prepared food are unhealthy. It's easy to serve your family good, homemade, nutritious meals in basically no time at all.

Making good, old-fashioned dinners is a huge contribution you can make to your family. Heating up chicken nuggets full of preservatives and chemicals and serving them with corn from a can is really a cop-out. Fry your kids some fresh chicken. It really doesn't take that much longer.

It's funny that many moms I know go out of their way to buy their kids the best designer clothes, yet they feed these kids the worst, cheapest-quality food. What's more important—what's on their bodies or what goes into them?

I hear women bragging that they don't cook, as if it's prestigious to be a lazy slob who gives her children processed junk. Really. I have girlfriends who just don't cook. I have no idea what their menus consist of, but I want to shake them. Who do they think they are? Why do they think they're too good to cook? Emeril Lagasse is a multimillionaire from cooking. The second love of my life, Bobby Flay, is a huge success from firing up the grill. And Martha Stewart has created an empire around her fluffy pancakes.

When we were children, we were raised with real down-home cooking. Our mothers spent time in the kitchen preparing dinner, and it was on the table every night. Why have the mothers of today forgotten this? I think moms today are so busy that they think they just don't have time to cook. Moms, you need to make the time. You need to give your children nutritious meals.

It's shocking to me how much junk food moms in America give their kids today. Is it any wonder little Johnny is jumping off the walls every night? Of course, you think you have to have him medicated—he's all junked up. Don't your children deserve to eat wholesome, nutritious meals? Don't you worry about what all that junk must be doing to your kids' bodies? Cut up some vegetables, throw in some meat, make a meal.

Cook for Your Family

You don't have to love to cook in order to prepare a quick, nutritious meal for the kids. I'll give you some easy ideas in this chapter—and please go to the bookstore. There are many cookbooks that specialize in recipes for moms on the go. If you aren't going to cook, at the very least you should pick up already prepared food that isn't terrible for you, such as fresh rotisserie chicken or a pizza. If you're lucky, you have a Whole Foods or a gourmet deli nearby where they produce fresh foods each day. Even I take a night off here and there and grab some prepared dishes from my local gourmet grocer, such as my favorite, grilled salmon cakes with couscous. I also visit my neighborhood Chinese restaurant a couple of times a month and get take-out. We have a great Tex-Mex place in town, and the chef uses the freshest ingredients. The children love the chicken tacos, and I, of course, love the margaritas. I think it costs about five dollars for a taco and seven dollars for the burrito that I get. Covered with fresh lettuce, tomato, beans, guacamole, and rice, it's much better and healthier than visiting Taco Bell. If you're taking the children out, why visit a fast-food place? Check out the other restaurants in your town.

If you don't mind cooking but are just terrible at it, like my sister, who recently made chicken Kiev that tasted like phlegm, please just try to follow a simple recipe. I have given her about a dozen cookbooks, but she tells me the recipes are too difficult, with way too many ingredients. So I started her on subscriptions to *Woman's Day, Ladies' Home Journal,* and *Martha Stewart Living,* and she really enjoys the recipes much more. She says they're much easier for her to follow. I think she's just not overwhelmed because there's a lot less choice and you can see the whole dinner on the page, photo and all. So, go for it—pick a recipe with fewer than ten ingredients and start cooking. If you mess it up, you can always make my favorite sandwich: peanut butter (crunchy, of course) and strawberry preserves.

I think a lot of moms become really desperate trying to figure out what to feed their families each day. If you start to look through the monthly magazines for ideas, I promise you'll find more than you could ever use. And remember to keep it simple. Like my sister, choose only recipes that you think you could re-create. You could cook a beautiful meal for your family with only a few ingredients.

One of my children's favorite dishes is my infamous chicken strips with honey dip. Easy. Take thick-sliced chicken cutlets and cut them into strips, dip in a beaten egg, then into bread crumbs, then into some grated Parmesan cheese and fry them in a little olive oil over medium heat, about four minutes per side. I usually use olive oil because it's healthier and I like the flavor it gives the meat. You can also put a little olive oil in a baking pan and bake these strips for about ten minutes on each side at 375°F. The strips should feel firm and have a nicely browned crust when done. For the dip, I mix equal parts of honey and Dijon mustard. This takes less than fifteen minutes, so what's the problem? Start cooking. I serve the chicken with raw baby carrots and sliced apples.

Yes, I am big on raw! I rarely cook my children's vegetables. I want them to have the full nutrients these foods offer. I give them a small cup of ranch dressing and they love to dip, even broccoli, which they won't even eat cooked. Let them nibble on some sliced veggies, such as red pepper, yellow zucchini, and little cherry tomatoes. Give them a bowl of that and some dip, maybe blue cheese, and watch them enjoy.

Some things I do cook, of course. Corn on the cob is one that my children really love.

There aren't a lot of nutrients in corn—it's mostly sugar—so it's a treat. Here's a quick tip, moms: Forget about peeling the husk. Dip it in water and throw it on the grill, turn over a few times, and in about twenty minutes it's done and more delicious that boiling.

The most important thing is to make your meals interesting and fun. I make mini-meatballs and put them on toothpicks, the ones with the fun colored ribbons at the end, with a bowl of ketchup for dipping. I slice my apples thin and tell the kids they're apple chips, just like potato chips. I slice up sweet potatoes and fry them in a little olive oil, sprinkle with salt, and my children love these French fries.

For my son's lunch, I make a sandwich and then press a cookie cutter into it. I send him off with these great shaped sandwiches, and his friends get a total kick out of them. I really think it's the little details that matter.

I can remember when I was a little girl—my mother is going to kill me for telling this story—and my best little girlfriend from school was coming over for lunch. I had recently been to her house for lunch, and her mom made us chicken noodle soup in cute little cups, tuna on toast that was cut in diagonals with the crust off, and, of course, big, gorgeous milkshakes. I loved that lunch. Then at my house, when Debbie sat down at my kitchen table, my mother flung two sandwiches onto the table, peanut butter and jelly with the biggest mom crime of all—mismatched bread. I was horrified. The slices were left whole, the crust was on, she didn't cut them in half. I was devastated. There was no soup in cute mugs and no special drink.

I remind my mother of this every so often. She never fussed. This infuriated me my entire life, and now I'm a compulsive fusser. Yes, I tie little bows around my napkins, make ribbons out of carrots, bake biscuits in the shape of bunnies, and make sure my pancakes stack up the same size. I'm a fusser and proud of it. I think a little extra fussing is a little extra love.

I must say this for my mother (or she'll never babysit for me again): She's a tremendous cook. She always prepared intricate meals, and she tries new recipes all the time. She always hosted huge holiday celebrations, and it was her recipes and example that I follow today. While our style of entertaining is different (I am way more uptight) she always put out a good table, which is what we say about women who serve a lot of great food. That is really important to my mother's side of the family—a lot of great homemade food on the table, more than could be eaten that night or for three nights.

This is how she was raised, with a folding table covered with trays of delicious home-made Italian food, and no one fussed or worried about how it looked, or how they looked eating it, for that matter. They had family, they had fun, and they enjoyed their food. This is an attitude I wish the ladies of my generation could adopt: enjoying food without guilt. And I know we don't want to look like my great-aunts, who were all over-weight, but at least they were happy and secure in themselves. We could all learn a lesson from them.

I never talk about dieting or watching what I eat in front of my children. I want them to enjoy food without guilt. I just don't have a lot of junk in the house, so it's not even an option for them. Tonight for dinner I made grilled swordfish, rice, broccoli, and carrots. They ate it. If you start when they're young, they'll grow up appreciating good food.

Your children could eat fresh fruits and veggies or cheese doodles and chips. It's a way of life, and it's up to you.

Don't get me wrong—my kids have their fix of junk now and then. Last week on a snow day I actually let them eat a whole bag of chips while they lounged around on the couch watching *Toy Story*, but I made sure they were preservative-free, natural potato chips, which taste fresher than the other kind anyway. You can find a healthier alternative to almost any food product at your health food store or online—check out Darla's Favorite Resources at the end of the book.

Speaking of health food stores, I am a big organic/holistic girl. I try my best to purchase locally produced, organic foods, especially dairy and meat. Once in a while we do fall off the wagon, I admit. Last week on a drive to Vermont we passed at least two million McDonald's along the thruway. Finally, I gave in and got my kids two Happy Meals, and yes, I ate some fries!

Listen, I know we cannot be perfect every second. But we can try our best. I believe that waking up and making your kids a batch of Mickey Mouse chocolate chip waffles from scratch is a gift they'll hold deep down for a lifetime. I think sharing dinners and talking about their day with Mom and Dad each night sets an example that will stay with them always.

Talk at the Table

This is a great way to get the scoop on your kids' lives. I heard a survey today on the radio about family vacations. The company who conducted the research asked children what their favorite memory of their favorite family vacation was, and the majority of the kids said it was eating with their parents. Can you believe that? *Eating with their parents.*

Now ladies, let's face it, most of us grew up in households where we sat down to dinner with our parents every night. We weren't overbooked. We didn't have all these extracurricular activities. Children today are on overdrive, coming and going all the time, and Mom spends much of her time driving the kids all over town. Who has time to sit down like a family anymore? The truth—and we all know this—is that the dinner table is one of the best spots to sit and bond with your children. The old-fashioned big family Sunday dinners are quickly becoming a thing of the past. Everyone is busy running off in different directions. I'm calling on all moms to start that tradition again. Make a Yankee pot roast. Invite the family, invite some friends. Being in the kitchen together, as a family, creates memories and tradition—on holidays especially. To me, half of the fun of the holidays is the baking, the cooking, the generations coming together to put a meal on the table.

Hearing about their day at school, talking about life, being together as a family—suppertime is important for the family. All of us, me included, have to start making sure that we bring back the art of this family dinner. I'm really guilty of this. I cook almost every night during the week because I want my children and I to eat good, nutritious foods, but I usually feed them at the island, and the television is on. Connor is usually doing his homework, and I may be on the phone or the computer. You know what? It's a bad habit that I have gotten myself into. Because my husband usually doesn't walk in the door until 8:00 or 9:00 P.M., we don't sit down at the table. It's just easier for me to feed them at the island.

This is no excuse. From now on I'm going to sit with them and talk. I'm going to shut off the television. My children are getting older now, and this is the perfect time to really get serious about this. I have to do this. So do you.

I make sure that on the weekends we always sit down to a family breakfast and dinner.

My husband usually grills, which he finds really relaxing, and we make sure that it's family time. On Sunday mornings I make fresh waffles or pancakes and we all sit around the kitchen table talking and looking through the papers. It's something my husband looks forward to all week. This family time at the table isn't just for the children; it's an opportunity for the whole family to be together. Even if you all go out to the pancake cottage on Sunday mornings, as long as you have this date together every weekend, you'll notice the difference.

Begin New Traditions

I'm sad that my grandmother Josephine is gone, because I just imagine the big Italian feasts we could have made together. I feel as if I'm missing out on something special, so I try my best to re-create these moments for my children. I bring them into the kitchen and have them help me prepare the special meals for our family. They love having a big feast, as they call it, when all of our family and our friends come to our home for a celebration. I'm trying to teach my children that this is what's important in life—not what you have, but how you live.

There are tiny honey balls called struffoli that Italians make around the holidays. You may have seen them in the grocery stores and the bakeries, but I assure you the store-bought kind tastes nothing like the light little creatures made from little old Italian ladies' hands. Anyway, weeks before Christmas, my aunt, my mother, my cousins, and I all gather to make a huge batch of this dessert (see the recipe on page 146). Obviously, it's a lot of work and we could just pick something up from the bakery, but the idea is to keep this tradition alive. And, of course, I believe food made from scratch always tastes better.

A lot of the women I know who were raised in very ethnic, traditional kitchens are just not re-creating the same dishes they were raised with. I know that we're very busy and on a daily basis I don't have time to prepare many detailed dishes; I rely on easy recipes on weeknights when I am rushing. But I try very hard on the weekends to keep alive some of the traditions I was raised with. I pull out the cookbooks, call the kids in, and spend many Sunday afternoons in my kitchen.

I cannot understand women saying that they hate to cook. I find it so therapeutic. Chopping, sautéing, drinking a glass of wine, being in my kitchen—I really enjoy it. If you have a mental block and think you're not cut out for the kitchen, please, just give it a few more chances. It's worth it for you and your family.

Have Fun!

Helping your children make homemade ice cream, freezing juice in the ice cube tray, making s'mores over the barbecue, icing a cake, putting an apron on and helping Mom in the kitchen, tasting real lemonade, and eating warm bread right out of the oven—these are the moments that your child really will remember. Think about your childhood. Think about your mother. Think about your grandmother. Think about all the little things that made your childhood great. I bet you'll remember some special days with your family, and I'm sure they'll include food.

One of my greatest memories is of staying at my grandparents' house in Massapequa, Long Island. My grandfather used to make me coffee in the morning (I was a young girl and it was about 10 percent coffee, 50 percent milk, and 40 percent sugar), and he would give me the best buttered roll, warm from the bakery up the block and filled with sweet homemade butter. I can still taste it to this day. It really wasn't the sweet cream of the butter or the sugar in the coffee that makes me remember those mornings. It was the time I spent with my grandparents that has left me with such wonderful memories. Just spending time with my grandparents was so special to me that I still cherish these memories. It was fun to be with them.

So bring your children over to Grandma's and bake some real, old-fashioned cookies from scratch. Let your kids ice the cookies and decorate them with sprinkles. Let your children mess up your kitchen. Let your children make you breakfast. You can always clean it up later, but you'll be giving them a great gift. Williams-Sonoma has some great ice cream makers and other fun things like heart-shaped pancake griddles and one of my favorites, a sandcastle Bundt pan that was a big hit over the summer. Take a look at www.williams-sonoma.com for more ideas.

Basic Cooking

You don't have to be afraid to go back to the kitchen. There are many cookbooks out there, but I'm only going to recommend a few to you. First, I want to give you a few tips. Start watching the Food Network and the cooking shows on PBS. Start paying attention to how the chefs cook. I'm not asking you to whip up gourmet meals for your family every day, but you can easily fry up some chicken cutlets instead of buying nuggets from the fast-food restaurant.

Make some salads—you can do that. Cut up some veggies and sauté them in a pan with a little olive oil and sliced garlic. Always add salt to everything while cooking. Don't be afraid to cook. You don't have to spend hours cooking, either. You could buy one or a few of Rachael Ray's cookbooks. She's a chef on the Food Network, and she specializes in meals that you can cook in thirty minutes. Check her out on www.foodnetwork.com.

I have dozens of cookbooks, and I love them. I doubt I'll ever feel satisfied until I own them all, but there's no reason you should have to buy that many. Do check out the cooking aisle at your bookstore, though—there are many great cookbooks that specialize in whatever it is that you're interested in. I just picked up one that's about sauces—100 great sauce and marinade recipes. Pick up a couple of books that focus on what you want. You know by now that my sister is not good in the kitchen, and I recently bought her *Cooking for Dummies* (Foster City, CA: IDG Books Worldwide, 1996). She needed to know how to make basic things like pancakes, eggs, pasta, and meat—easy, everyday recipes. If you don't have time to look through cookbooks or the money to spend on them, there are numerous websites where you can look up recipes for free and in just a few seconds. Just type what you want to make in your search engine and a host of recipes will pop up. Check out these sites in Darla's Favorite Resources in the back of this book. If you're a member of AOL (America Online), which I just love, take a look at AOL Food, with helpful daily recipes. As you know, I keep my laptop in my kitchen on the island, and I look each morning for recipes to make for dinner. Also, most of the magazines that I want you to start reading are full of recipes. I rip them out each month and tape them to the inside of my cabinets. I shop for the ingredients and try new recipes each week. All of these magazines have coordinating websites where you can find the recipes. I love looking through the pages with a cup of tea; it's very relaxing. My favorite recipe sources are:

Cooking Light	*www.cookinglight.com*
Southern Living	*www.southernliving.com*
Martha Stewart Living	*www.marthastewart.com*
Good Housekeeping	*www.goodhousekeeping.com*
Ladies' Home Journal	*www.lhj.com*

Each of these magazines provides monthly themed dishes and seasonal recipes. Flip through the pages, rip out what you want to make, and put them into a folder. I've created my own cookbooks of my favorite recipes that I have ripped out. I especially love the photos. I would rather cook something if I can see what it should look like when it's completed.

Martha Stewart has just come out with a kids' magazine, *Martha Stewart Kids*. I really like it because it gives me a lot of ideas to prepare foods in ways that will be attractive to my children.

As I mentioned earlier, I love to press cookie cutters into my son's sandwich in the morning. He gets a kick out of this and so do his friends. So the next time you want to make your son the usual turkey on white bread, press a bug shape into it, which also cuts the crusts off, and see how much life you bring to that sandwich. You can get cookie cutters anywhere, but you can order really fun shapes at www.cookiecutter.com, www.kitchengifts.com, and www.candylandcrafts.com.

I've come up with some pretty creative ways to sneak nutrition into my children's bodies. I keep my blender, juicer, and Cuisinart on my counter, and I'm always throwing fresh herbs, vegetables, fruit, and whatever I can into those machines. Once it's chopped, squeezed, and blended together, the children have no idea what they're eating. As I mentioned, I throw plain vanilla yogurt, strawberries, a banana, and some orange juice into the blender with a few ice cubes and the children think they're drinking an ice cream shake. I take an apple, some carrots, and some fresh spinach and throw it into the juicer, and the children have a nutritious, healthy drink.

Juicing is just about the best way to give your children the natural vitamins and nutrition they need. When you cook vegetables, they lose some nutrients. Plus, there's no way you're going to get your children to eat a big bowl full of spinach. If you take that spinach and juice it with some sweet fruits, such as apples, or strawberries, or even carrots, it becomes a yummy drink. I tell my children that it's the monster drink or the Shrek drink, and they love it.

I have a few books on juicing and making smoothies. You'll need to buy a juicer, and there are smoothie makers you can buy now instead of regular blenders. I have a Champion juicer and a Back-to-Basics smoothie maker. To purchase these machines, visit www.livingright.com or www.everythingkitchens.com.

Juicing

First of all, use common sense—throw some oranges or grapes into the juicer, whatever fruit and veggies you want, and there you have it—fresh juice. I slice up a watermelon with the rind and drink it up (if you're constipated, this will do the trick). I just cannot recommend this fresh juice thing enough. Many parents give their children juice all day long. First of all, please remember that they need water. Fresh, purified water is essential and healthy for your child. When you give your baby juice, do you want to give him juice with sugar? Do you want to give your child juice that has been sitting in a plastic container for months? I don't. I know we're all busy, and of course you'll sometimes give your child juice on the go, but hopefully it will be organic juice without pesticides in it. When you're at home, why not make your child some fresh apple juice? Think about it. It takes a little more time out of your day, but isn't it worth it? For some juice recipes, visit www.healthrecipes.com.

Smoothies

This, too, is not a science. Just throw in a bunch of fresh fruit, some milk, yogurt, and some ice and turn on the machine. You can also use frozen fruit mixed with milk. It's really yummy, and your children will ask for it, I promise. For some delicious ideas, visit www.cdkitchen.com.

The bottom line: Give it a shot. You want your children to live long, healthy lives and what you give them now will partly determine whether they will be fat, thin, healthy, or sickly in the future. It's irresponsible to allow your children to eat doughnuts, bagged junk, frozen foods, and soda all day without any fresh fruits, vegetables, or homemade meals. America has the fattest kids and the fattest adults, we buy the most junk food, and we're a bunch of lazy slobs. It's time to stop. It's time to teach your children healthy eating habits. It's time for you to get your act together—it's your responsibility to feed your family. You're the mother. Now stop this nonsense and start preparing some decent meals for your children. You just might enjoy it.

This morning my butcher gave me a recipe that I am going to make tonight. On page 109 is what I'll be cooking; from my kitchen to yours.

PEPPERED FLANK STEAK

6 SERVINGS

1½-pound lean flank steak

1 teaspoon cracked or freshly ground black pepper

1 garlic clove, minced

¼ teaspoon kosher salt

1 teaspoon olive oil

1 tablespoon balsamic vinegar

2 tablespoons fresh lemon juice

1. Rub the steak with the pepper and salt.
2. In a skillet heat the oil on medium-high heat. Add the garlic and steak. Pour the vinegar over the steak and cook about 5 minutes on each side or until the steak is done to your liking.
3. Cut the steak across the grain into thin slices. Drizzle the lemon juice over the steak and serve.

Sounds easy! I'll let you know how it tastes. . . .

It's yummy—good! I sliced up some potatoes, tossed them with a tablespoon of olive oil, kosher salt, and some garlic powder, and baked them at 375°F for thirty minutes. I served this along with a salad with chopped avocado, some oil, and vinegar, and it was a great dinner. I put some of the steak into a wrap and sprinkled cheese over it and gave that to the children. They loved it.

As you know, I have a lot of cookbooks, magazines, and family recipes accumulated in my kitchen. I try to mix up what I make to be a little creative so that it doesn't get boring. I love to cook. It's my favorite pastime next to eating. So, I'm going to give you a few of my favorite recipes along with some tips to make your life easier and to help you to feel more comfortable in the kitchen.

Most of the recipes that I've cut out of magazines, stolen from girlfriends, or learned from my mother are piled up in my junk drawer. Most of them I re-create by heart. But if I'm making something special for an occasion or company, I've learned by trial and error that I have to follow exact directions. I've skipped through a recipe too quickly and ruined the whole meal. Make sure you read the directions before you begin. Sometimes the recipe will call for six eggs, and you beat them all together only to learn that one egg was intended to glaze the top of the pie at the end.

It's important to enjoy the process. If you have twenty people coming for dinner, why try a new recipe that day? You're asking for a disaster. Stick with dishes that you know will come out well. And please remember that it's perfectly acceptable to mix store-bought and homemade foods. Sometimes when I have the girls over for lunch I buy a rotisserie chicken, shred the meat, and place it over salad greens along with sliced avocado, cherry tomatoes, Bermuda onions, and broken-up blue corn tortilla chips. I top it with a homemade dressing that I mix from ¼ cup of olive oil, 1 teaspoon of stone-ground mustard, 1 tablespoon of honey, a squeeze of fresh lime juice, a dash of kosher salt, some fresh pepper, and chopped fresh cilantro. Pour the dressing over the salad right before company shows up. You could make this really quickly if you use premade salad dressing—for this salad I suggest Ken's Steak House brand Lite Raspberry Walnut Vinaigrette—although homemade dressing tastes much better.

Remember, your family needs good, nutritious food every day, so try to buy the freshest ingredients for your meal. If a recipe calls for fresh basil, don't use the dried-up version. Fresh herbs, kosher salt, good olive oil, freshly ground pepper, and seasonal fruits and vegetables will transform the meal.

Always remember to flavor your food. Salt—kosher salt, sea salt—it does matter. (I'm a big kosher salt girl.) Read the directions, and when you're winging it, remember you should almost always add salt. When you make pasta, you must put salt in the water for taste. When you make eggs, a dash of kosher salt in the beaten eggs will transform the flavor, and remember to add salt to your meat before you cook.

Mostly, though, I just cook with common sense. A little bit of this and a little bit of that.

Important Cooking Tips

- Always buy organic food when you can. Most of the food grocery carry organic chicken, such as Bell & Evans, and organic meat, such as Coleman's, so try to buy this to avoid putting unnecessary hormones in your children's little bodies.
- Ground meat: I try to buy chopped sirloin because it's leaner.
- Always wash your chicken before cooking. Soak it in a pot with some kosher salt for about five minutes to clean it of any yucky stuff. Make sure you rinse the inside of a whole chicken, and check for any bags of chicken parts or plastic pieces, especially with a turkey. There's always a bag of giblets hiding in the cavity. Pat the chicken dry with paper towels before cooking.
- Speaking of patting dry, when you're going to fry something, make sure you dry it before putting it into a pan of hot oil or the oil will splash out and give you a very messy, greasy stove.
- Always wash your fruits and vegetables. Soak your lettuce in a pot of water, and then drain it in a salad spinner. Sometimes I have to soak and rinse my fresh spinach three times before the water is clean. Don't skip this step. Nothing is worse than biting into a gritty, dirty salad. I recently complained in a restaurant after biting into a grilled portabella mushroom and feeling sand between my teeth. Yuck!

- A lot of the best nutrients are found in the skin of fruits, so carefully wash the dirt off and enjoy. I fill a pot up with about six cups of cold water, two tablespoons of white vinegar, and a squeeze of fresh lemon juice to clean my fruits and veggies. The vinegar and lemon are natural cleansers. Some people buy a vegetable cleaning solution, but I prefer this all-natural method, which is also a lot cheaper.

- Vinegar is a great product, by the way. It's cheap and does many things. If you wash down your patio in the spring with white vinegar, green mold won't grow. Visit www.heloise.com for more vinegar ideas.

- For salads, use extra-virgin olive oil or flaxseed oil. For sautéing food over medium heat, use regular olive oil. For high-heat frying or deep frying, use vegetable oil. I prefer canola oil over corn oil.

- Keep a can of olive oil spray, vegetable oil spray, and baking spray in your pantry for quick coating.

- I recommend using All-Clad or heavy stainless steel pans at all times for the stove and in the oven. I like glass and sometimes nonstick pans for baking. I have a small Teflon pan I use for making eggs and a Teflon skillet I use for pancakes. I have never had much success making pancakes or omelets in metal pans because they always stick to the bottom. Spray the Teflon with your canned oil or use a pat of butter. Remember to cook on medium heat when using Teflon. It cannot tolerate high heat—it gives off fumes that can make you sick—and you must use wooden utensils so you don't scratch the surface.

- I really love all the new freezer-to-table products. They come in so many cute colors. You could bake a meal, put it on the table, and put the leftovers into the freezer all with one pan. Emile Henry makes a great product, and you can find it on www.surlatable.com.

- Buy Parmesan cheese fresh from your deli department. They'll grate it for you if you don't want to do it yourself.

- Remember to flavor your food. If you throw a turkey in the oven it will be terribly boring and tasteless if you don't add seasonings. You should rub salt and pepper into any meat you make before cooking. When I roast a turkey, I lift the skin and slide chunks of butter under it. I have also stuffed apricot marmalade under the skin. Just remember to add flavor—fresh herbs, garlic, and onions—to spice it up a bit.

- There are many varieties of seasonings, marinades, sauces, gravies, and ready-made food kits; all you need to do is smother any meat or add to pasta and you have a meal. Pick up some of Chef Paul's flavors, Emeril's Essence, McCormick packets, or Annie's Marinades, and most of your work is already done for you.

- When you're cooking something, as soon as you scoop the food out of the pan, pour an inch or two of water into it while the heat is still on. It will lift the layer of gunk off the bottom of the pan, and clean-up will be a breeze.

- Clean up as you go. I cannot stress this enough. It's hard to enjoy a meal when you're plagued with knowing you have a dirty kitchen to tend to— especially when you're having company. Prepare it all ahead of time and let them see a clean kitchen and a hostess in control, and you'll have a much better time.

Last Sunday, I had a few couples over with their children. I prepared vegetable lasagna and a tray of chicken marsala the day before. Earlier that day, I prepared a salad. When they arrived, my trays were in the oven heating up, the salad was sitting pretty on the counter in a beautiful bowl, and the only thing on my kitchen island was a big, gorgeous antipasto. I set out a huge platter; on it I put a bunch of prepared deli items: olives, mozzarella cheese, pepperoni slices, marinated peppers, a cheese spread, gourmet crackers, celery slices, and artichoke hearts. For the cocktails I made a huge pitcher of sangria with sliced apples and grapes in it for color. Easy. You can do this!

There are about a thousand recipes I'd like to recommend to you, but there's no way I could add them all now, so I'm just going to give you some of my favorites.

· Breakfast ·

This is my absolute favorite meal, so I'm always coming up with new things to make and eat.

Pancakes

The perfect comfort food. There's nothing better than sitting down to a big batch of fluffy pancakes in your jammies. All children love this. On weekends or holidays I go on-line and get recipes for pancakes to make from scratch. For a great selection, go to www.mrbreakfast.com.

I have to admit that most days I take a shortcut and use Bisquick. I add mashed bananas, whole blueberries, or small chocolate chips to the pancake recipe on the box, and the children love it. I never skimp and always use 100 percent pure maple syrup. Yes, it costs more, but it's the real thing and you can totally taste the difference.

FRENCH TOAST

· · · · · · · · · · · · · · ·

4 SLICES (2 SERVINGS)

This is Hannah's favorite.

2 eggs
2 tablespoons milk
A few shakes of cinnamon
Pinch of nutmeg
½ teaspoon vanilla
1 tablespoon butter
4 slices cinnamon swirl bread
Powered sugar
Sliced strawberries

1. In a medium bowl, beat together eggs, milk, cinnamon, nutmeg, and vanilla. Dip a slice of bread in the mixture, quickly coating each side.

2. In a large frying pan, heat the butter over medium-high heat. Place the bread in the pan and cook for about 4 minutes, turning once, until both sides are slightly brown. You may place more than one slice of bread in the pan at a time, as long as they do not have to touch each other.

3. Top the finished toast with the powdered sugar and sliced strawberries, and serve.

MY FAMOUS EGGS

Connor loves these eggs, and they're really simple to make. Just be sure not to overcook the eggs. Bill always makes them way too dry. The trick is to take them off the heat as soon as they're fully formed.

4 large eggs
1 tablespoon milk or cream
Nice dash of kosher salt
Handful of shredded Mexican cheese
1 tablespoon butter

In a medium bowl, lightly beat the eggs, milk or cream, salt, and cheese. Heat the butter in a frying pan over medium-high heat. Add the egg mixture and scramble.

· Lunch ·

I try to sneak some nutrition and fun into lunch. Remember to buy those cookie cutters. The fun shapes get the children chomping. Even peanut butter and jelly tastes better when it's shaped like a star.

Hannah loves peanut butter and sliced banana sandwiches. I buy organic peanut butter. Use any kind of bread your children prefer.

Connor loves macaroni and cheese. It's so easy. I cook 1 pound of elbow macaroni, drain it, and add ¼ stick of butter to it, and ½ cup of shredded cheddar cheese. Mix it together while the pasta is hot, and it all melts wonderfully.

My favorite lunch sandwich is easy: turkey breast slices on white bread with a slice of Granny Smith apple, a slice of provolone cheese, and a light smear of mayonnaise.

MY FAMOUS CHICKEN SALAD

4 SERVINGS

This is Bill's favorite.

2 cups small chicken chunks
¹⁄₂ cup celery slices
¹⁄₄ cup shredded carrots
³⁄₄ cup mayonnaise
¹⁄₄ teaspoon salt
¹⁄₄ teaspoon pepper
¹⁄₂ cup dried cranberries (I use Ocean Spray)
Pita bread

1. Buy a rotisserie chicken, or boil your own (I buy four chicken breasts). In a medium soup pot bring 8 cups of water with 1 tablespoon of salt to a boil and add chicken. Lower the heat to medium-high and cook for 15 to 20 minutes. Check to see if the chicken is fully cooked by cutting into the thickest part of the meat to see if it is white. When cooked through, remove the chicken from the water and set it aside to cool. Peel the meat off the chicken and break it into small pieces.

2. Place the chicken pieces in a medium bowl. Add the celery, carrots, mayonnaise, salt, pepper, and cranberries and mix thoroughly. Stuff the mixture into small pita breads.

FUN PASTA

6 TO 8 KID-SIZE SERVINGS

3 tablespoons olive oil

¼ cup green zucchini, diced

¼ cup yellow zucchini, diced

¼ cup red pepper, diced

¼ cup yellow pepper, diced

2 small garlic cloves, sliced

1 pound fusilli pasta, cooked and drained

¼ cup freshly grated Parmesan cheese

1. In a large sauté pan, heat the olive oil over medium heat. Add the zucchini and peppers and sauté until they begin to soften, about 2 minutes. Add the garlic and sauté until softened, about three minutes.

2. Stir in the pasta and serve with Parmesan sprinkled on top.

MINI PIZZA

Make as many of these as you need. My father made them almost every night of my childhood.

For each pizza: Toast an English muffin to firm it up. Spoon a couple of teaspoons of jarred tomato sauce (I prefer Paul Newman's Five Cheese Sauce) onto the muffin, covering the top. (Don't use too much sauce or the muffins will be soggy.) Sprinkle shredded mozzarella cheese on top. Bake at 400°F until the cheese is bubbly and starting to brown, about 8 minutes.

PIGS IN A BLANKET

· ·

8 SERVINGS

These are easy to make, and the children get a kick out of putting them together. Serve with bowls of ketchup and mustard for dipping.

8 hot dogs (I prefer nitrate-free Coleman's or Apple Gate Farms), sliced in half crosswise to make mini-dogs
1 package refrigerated biscuit or croissant dough (I prefer Pillsbury)

1. Preheat the oven to 350°F and lightly grease a baking sheet.
2. Wrap each hot dog piece with a piece of dough, leaving the ends exposed. Use one biscuit for each half dog.
3. Place the wrapped dogs on the sheet, seam-side down. Bake 10 to 15 minutes, or until the biscuit is golden brown.

· Quick Dinner Ideas ·

Spaghetti and Meatballs

This is a touchy subject for Italian people. My mother's family is always arguing over who makes the best sauce and the best meatballs, and, believe me, the competition never ends.

I'm now part of the debate, and, of course, I think I make the best meatballs and sauce. Every time my mother is over and eats my food, she has something to say about it. "Did you put onions in these meatballs?" She knows damn well I did, but she just has to aggravate me. She also goes crazy over how I make my sauce. She's from the old school and lets her meat cook in the sauce all day on the stove. I think that's unnecessary, and I cook my sauce for only an hour, and you know what? It's pretty delicious.

Oh, and there are so many people now baking their meatballs—no way! There's nothing better than a nice, greasy meatball right out of the frying pan. There are some things that shouldn't be changed. And ladies, it's not the fried meatball keeping the pounds on your ass—it's eating too many of them. So enjoy the real thing the right way, and just don't eat them all yourself.

DARLA'S MEATBALLS

· ·

8 SERVINGS

2 slices white sandwich bread cut up into little pieces

½ cup plain bread crumbs (I buy 4C)

2 pounds ground sirloin

A generous ½ cup grated Parmesan cheese

¼ cup chopped fresh parsley

2 teaspoons kosher salt

½ medium onion, diced

½ cup milk

2 large eggs, beaten

Freshly ground black pepper

Olive oil for frying

1. Place all the ingredients except the olive oil in a large bowl. Wash your hands and use them to combine the mixture thoroughly. Yes, this is cold and gross, but it's the best way to do it.

2. Form the mixture into 1½-inch balls, place them on a plate, cover them in plastic wrap, and refrigerate for about 15 minutes so they harden a bit and don't fall apart in the pan.

3. Pour olive oil ¼ inch deep into a large frying pan and heat the oil to medium-high. Add the meatballs and fry, turning them carefully until they're crispy and brown on all sides. Fill up the pan with the balls, keeping some room to turn them. I can fit them all in my huge pan, but you may have to fry them in batches. Add more oil if you need it for the second batch, but be sure to heat it before you add the meatballs.

4. Drain on paper towels.

NOTE: Sometimes for the children I put the meatballs onto hot dog buns and cover with ketchup. They enjoy this. Most of the time, though, it's old-fashioned spaghetti and meatballs.

Like I said, my mother, a real Italian, stuck to her roots and cooks the sauce (which *real* Italians call "gravy") all day long. The meat soaks in the gigantic pot, bubbling all day Sunday until the family arrives. Who has time for that? I can make a pot of sauce, meatballs, and spaghetti and have it all on the table within an hour. So here's what I do . . .

DARLA'S QUICKIE SAUCE

· ·

8 SERVINGS

3 tablespoons olive oil

1 small yellow onion, chopped

2 large garlic cloves, chopped

2 28-ounce cans crushed tomatoes

1 teaspoon kosher salt

1. Pour the olive oil into a large sauté pan. Heat over medium-high heat until the olive oil begins to liquefy. Add the onions, and sauté until softened. Add the garlic, and sauté until golden. Slowly add in the tomatoes and the salt.

2. Bring the sauce to a boil and turn the heat to low. Add the meatballs and cook, stirring often with—and this is a must—a big wooden spoon. The sauce will be done in 30 minutes.

While the sauce is cooking, boil a pot of water. Read the directions on the side of the pasta box. In our house the children are huge angel hair pasta fans, so I make that a lot. Be sure you do two things: salt your water thoroughly (for one pound of spaghetti cooked in half a pot of boiling water, add two teaspoons of kosher salt), and don't overcook your pasta. Nothing is worse than mushy pasta. You want it soft but firm. Read the directions on the box for cooking time, but always do a taste test. After you drain the pasta, add a few spoonfuls of your sauce to it and stir to keep it from sticking together.

Pour the pasta into a big bowl, spoon some sauce and meatballs over it, and sprinkle freshly chopped basil, cracked pepper, and Parmesan cheese on top and you have a great, fresh Italian dinner ready within one hour.

PORK CHOPS

· · · · · · · · · · · · · · ·

4 SERVINGS

Here's my mother's recipe. Buy the chops with the bone on—they stay juicier that way. Try to get a nice size pork chop, about 1½ inches thick.

1. Dip both sides of the pork chop in red vinegar, then into breadcrumbs, and fry in olive oil over medium heat on both sides until the pork chops are nice and crispy, about 6 minutes per side. Make sure that you cover the pan while cooking so that the meat virtually bakes through. Don't overcook or they will be hard as a rock.

2. You can also coat a baking pan with olive oil and put the pork chops in the oven for about 40 minutes at 350°F, turning over halfway through. Always check that your pork is cooked through. (Never eat pork or chicken that is pink in the middle.)

3. Smother the chops with apple sauce, which the kids love. Easy enough, right?

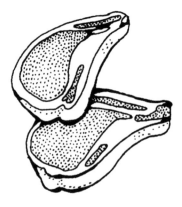

BEST RIBS IN THE WORLD

My cousin Linda gave me this recipe.

Buy a rack of pork baby back ribs. Bring them to a boil in 2 liters of Coca-Cola—yes, that's right. Be careful, this is messy! Use a really big pot. Once it's boiling, you can lower the heat to medium to keep it from bubbling over. Cook on medium heat for 2 hours. Then remove ribs and place them on the grill and slather your favorite barbecue sauce on top. Grill on high for 5 to 8 minutes per side or until nicely crisp with some black edges. Wait until you taste these—I promise you'll go crazy for them!

MY STEAK AND ONION SANDWICHES

4 SERVINGS

3 large yellow onions, thinly sliced

3 tablespoons olive oil

2 teaspoons kosher salt

1 pound thinly sliced flank steak

1 tablespoon butter

¼ tablespoon pepper

4 club rolls

8 slices cheddar cheese

4 tablespoons barbecue sauce

1. Heat the olive oil in a medium pan over medium-high heat. Add the onions and salt and sauté the onions until they're caramelized (soft and slightly brown), about 10 minutes. Set the onions aside on a plate.

2. Add the butter and flank steak to the pan and sprinkle salt and pepper to taste on top. Cook over medium-high heat for 5 minutes, or until the meat is browned on the outside but slightly pink in the middle. Set the steak aside with the onions.

3. Open the sandwich rolls for each serving and place them in the pan over low heat to toast for a minute or two.

4. Place the steak and onions in each sandwich and add a slice of cheese if you like. Top with barbecue sauce.

CHILI/TACOS

* * * * * * * * * * * * * *

6 SERVINGS

There are a thousand ways to make chili, and this is my version. I use a McCormick chili mild seasoning mix. You can use this exact recipe using McCormick taco seasoning and make tacos for the children. Just line up bowls of cheese, lettuce, chopped tomatoes, sour cream, and tortillas and let the kids have fun making their own tacos. I also like to make a big pot of white rice. Put some into a bowl, scoop some chili on top, and add black beans, sliced green onions, and sour cream for my mile-high chili feast.

1 teaspoon olive oil

1 yellow onion, chopped

1 green pepper, chopped

1 garlic clove, chopped

1½ pounds ground sirloin

1 can crushed tomatoes

1 packet McCormick chili seasoning

1 can red kidney beans, rinsed and
   drained

1 can baked beans

1 teaspoon salt

1. In a large saucepan or Dutch oven, heat the olive oil over medium heat. Add the onion and green pepper, and sauté until softened. Add the garlic and ground sirloin, and sauté until the meat is browned. Drain the meat mixture in a colander.

2. Wipe the pan down with paper towels and place the meat mixture back into the pan. Add the crushed tomatoes, chili seasoning, kidney beans, baked beans, and salt. Simmer over low heat for an hour, or until the chili has reached the desired consistency.

FAJITAS

4 SERVINGS

I love to make fajitas, and the children love to eat them. They taste better if you make them in an iron skillet. Williams-Sonoma carries fajita seasoning, or look for it in the spice section of your grocery store. McCormick also makes a great fajita seasoning mix.

1 pound sliced chicken or beef
3 tablespoons fajita seasoning (or
    depending on which seasoning
    packet you buy; check the direc-
    tions)
1 red pepper, sliced

1 green pepper, sliced
1 red onion, sliced
2 garlic cloves, sliced
3 tablespoons olive oil
White flour tortillas
Sour cream

1. Place the meat, fajita seasoning, and water (per package instructions) in a large bowl, cover, and marinate for 30 minutes in the refrigerator.
2. In a large sauté pan, heat the olive oil over medium heat. Add the peppers, onion, and garlic, and sauté until softened. Add the marinated meat.
3. Raise the heat to high and get that pan sizzling. Stir with a wooden spoon, scraping the bottom to get the best flavors.
4. When the pan gets sticky and the sauce gets thick, add a tablespoon of water and mix and scrape more. Cook the fajitas about 10 minutes in all, or until the meat is browned and the chicken is firm and done.
5. Wrap the fajita mixture in the tortillas and serve with sour cream on the side.

KIDS' PASTA

6 SERVINGS

I make this at least twice a week—the children love it and it's *soooo* easy.

1 bunch broccoli, cut into florets
½ teaspoon kosher salt
1 pound pasta (your child's favorite)
3 tablespoons olive oil
3 garlic cloves, sliced
2 tablespoons freshly grated Parmesan cheese

1. Bring a large pot of water to a boil over high heat with the salt. Add the broccoli and blanch for 2 minutes, or until slightly softened. Use a slotted spoon to remove it to a bowl.

2. Add the pasta to the broccoli water and cook until al dente, stirring often. Drain the pasta.

3. Meanwhile, in a large sauté pan, heat the olive oil. Add the garlic, and sauté until it softens and browns slightly, about 2 minutes.

4. To serve, place the pasta in a big bowl, put the garlic on top, add the broccoli, mix together, and sprinkle with Parmesan cheese.

ZUCCHINI BOATS

My children had this dish as an appetizer at a restaurant, and now they ask for it. It's a good way to sneak a vegetable in.

4 small zucchini, washed and sliced in half lengthwise, seeds scooped out
½ cup jarred tomato sauce
1 cup shredded mozzarella

1. Preheat the oven to 350°F.
2. Fill each zucchini with a little tomato sauce and a lot of shredded mozzarella cheese.
3. Place the zucchini in a baking pan coated with olive oil spray and bake 20 minutes, or until the zucchini is tender and the cheese is melted.

SLOPPY JOES

. . . .

4 SERVINGS

Connor and his friends go crazy for these, and they're really simple to make. Serve with potato chips (Yoghurt and Green Onion Kettle Chips are our favorite) and pickles.

1 pound ground sirloin
¼ teaspoon kosher salt
1 cup ketchup
¼ cup brown sugar
1 tablespoon molasses
4 hamburger buns

1. In a large sauté pan, brown the sirloin over medium heat. Add the salt to the meat as it's cooking. Once it's no longer pink, drain the meat and add the ketchup.
2. Mix 1 cup of water with the brown sugar, and pour the mixture into the pan. Cook a few minutes over medium heat until the water starts to evaporate. Add the molasses and cook on low for 15 minutes, or until the sauce is creamy.
3. Serve the mixture on the hamburger buns.

ALL-IN-THE-PAN CHICKEN

6 SERVINGS

I love this dish. I just throw it in the oven and bake it for an hour at 350°F.

1 chicken, cut into 8 pieces

3 tablespoons olive oil

Juice of 1 lemon

1 lemon, thinly sliced

½ cup freshly chopped basil

½ cup freshly chopped parsley

1 large yellow onion, sliced

3 garlic cloves, sliced

2 celery sticks, sliced

3 carrots, sliced

6 small red potatoes, cut in halves

1 teaspoon kosher salt

Freshly ground black pepper

½ cup Parmesan cheese

1. Preheat the oven to 350°F.

2. Wash and place the chicken in the large roasting pan or Dutch oven. Add the olive oil and mix to coat. Squeeze a lemon over the chicken and place the lemon slices in the pan. Add the basil, parsley, onion, garlic, celery, carrots, potatoes, salt, and pepper. Mix thoroughly to coat with the olive oil and seasonings.

3. Cover with aluminum foil and roast for 30 minutes. Stir the chicken and vegetables and roast, uncovered, for 15 minutes. If the potatoes are soft, scoop them out so they don't get too mushy. Roast the chicken for 15 minutes more, or until golden brown and cooked through.

4. Serve with a sprinkling of Parmesan cheese over each serving.

FILLET OF FISH

4 TO 6 SERVINGS

1 pound flounder or tilapia fillets
½ cup milk
2 eggs, beaten
½ cup bread crumbs
2 tablespoons canola oil
Tartar sauce (see Note below)

1. Cut the fillets into pieces no more than 4 inches long, or you'll have trouble flipping them in the pan. Dip the fish fillets in milk and wipe with a paper towel. Dip next in the beaten egg and then the bread crumbs.

2. In a large sauté pan, heat the canola oil over medium-high heat. Add the fillets and fry about 3 minutes per side, or until golden and crispy. Serve with tartar sauce.

NOTE: You can make a quick, delicious tartar sauce from ½ cup mayonnaise, a squeeze of fresh lemon, and a forkful of relish.

CHICKEN FRIED RICE

4 SERVINGS (OR ONE, BECAUSE I USUALLY EAT IT ALL MYSELF)

I love my fried rice—I think it's better than at a restaurant. I like to add a spoonful of duck sauce on top.

2 cups cooked white rice (I prefer Carolina's long grain)
3 tablespoons peanut oil
1 small white onion, diced
1 carrot, sliced
1 leek, sliced (omit the very white and very dark green parts)
2 small chicken breast cutlets, sliced into thin strips
3 tablespoons soy sauce
½ teaspoon sugar
1 cup frozen baby peas
2 eggs, beaten

1. In a large sauté pan, heat 2 tablespoons of the peanut oil over medium heat. Add the onion and start to sauté. Add the carrot, leek, and chicken and sauté until the chicken is browned.
2. Add 2 tablespoons of the soy sauce, the sugar, and the peas. Stir with a wooden spoon until everything starts to brown. Pour it all into a big bowl.
3. Add the remaining 1 tablespoon of soy sauce and the eggs to the pan.
4. Scramble quickly over medium-high heat, cutting the egg into small pieces, and add to the mixture in the bowl.
5. Add the remaining 1 tablespoon of peanut oil to the pan over medium-high heat. Add the rice and stir quickly.
6. When the rice starts to brown a bit, add the mixture from the bowl into the pan. Stir it to combine, and serve.

SWORDFISH WITH MANGO SALSA

....

4 SERVINGS

Just about every time I have company in the summer I make this dish. It's best to make it in summer when all the ingredients are the freshest. Serve with couscous, page 138.

For the salsa:

2 ripe mangos, peeled and cut into small pieces

1 ripe large white peach (no need to peel) washed and cut into small ½-inch pieces

1 medium ripe tomato, diced

1 tablespoon chopped fresh cilantro

1 tablespoon fresh lime juice

1 tablespoon honey

For the swordfish:

4 medium swordfish steaks

1 cup Newman's Own Family Recipe Italian dressing

1. To make the salsa: Combine all the ingredients in a medium bowl, cover, and refrigerate until needed.

2. To make the swordfish: Marinate the swordfish in the dressing for 30 minutes, covered, in the refrigerator. Preheat the grill to high. Grill the swordfish for 5 minutes per side, or until firm through and nicely charred. Serve with the salsa on top of the swordfish, and couscous on the side.

MY COUSCOUS

· · · · · · · · · · · · · · · · · ·

4 SERVINGS

This couscous is famous, at least within my family. A lot of people don't know about couscous, and it's really a great side dish. I start with a boxed mix—I prefer Near East couscous, the toasted pine nut flavor—but I jazz it up a bit.

1 tablespoon olive oil
1 leek, sliced
1 sweet potato, sliced into thin ½-inch pieces
1 box Near East couscous
Chicken broth (optional)
1 small Granny Smith apple, diced

In a medium sauté pan, heat the olive oil over medium heat. Add the leek and sweet potato and cook until softened. Add the seasoning packet and recommended cups of water, or chicken broth, if you prefer. Add the couscous, stir, and remove from the heat. Stir in the apple and serve.

· My Favorite Soups ·

SQUASH SOUP
••••••••••••••••

6 SERVINGS

I don't remember how I came up with this, but I played around a bit, and my family loves the results.

1 leek, sliced

2 tablespoons olive oil

1 teaspoon kosher salt

1 shallot, chopped

2 cups 1-inch pieces of peeled butternut squash

2 cups 1-inch pieces of peeled sweet potato

1 carrot, sliced

1 Granny Smith apple, sliced

1 teaspoon ground ginger

6 cups chicken broth (preferably Imagine Organic free-range chicken broth)

2 tablespoons fresh parsley, chopped

2 tablespoons fresh sage, thinly sliced

1. In a big soup pot or Dutch oven, sauté the leek in the olive oil over medium heat until translucent. Add the salt, shallot, squash, sweet potato, carrot, and apple, and sauté the mixture until softened. Add the ginger, chicken broth, and parsley. Turn the heat to low and simmer for 30 minutes. If it gets too thick, add 1 to 2 cups of water.

2. Pour the mixture into a Cuisinart or blender and blend until smooth. You'll most likely have to do this in two batches.

3. Serve in bowls with croutons and a few strips of thinly sliced fresh sage on top.

VEGETABLE SOUP

I make this a lot in the winter; it's very healthy for the kids.

2 teaspoons olive oil

1 cup chopped yellow onion

2 garlic cloves, chopped

2 celery stalks, sliced

2 carrots, sliced

1 potato, peeled and diced

1 leek, sliced

¾ teaspoon kosher salt

½ teaspoon freshly ground black
　pepper

3 cups chicken broth

1 tablespoon fresh basil, chopped

1 tablespoon fresh parsley, chopped

1 16-ounce can cannelloni beans or
　other white beans, drained

1 16-ounce can whole tomatoes, not
　drained, chopped

½ cup elbow macaroni

½ cup shredded mozzarella

1. In a medium soup pot or Dutch oven, heat the olive oil over medium heat. Add the onion, garlic, celery, carrots, potato, leek, salt, and pepper, and sauté until slightly softened and browned.

2. Add 4 cups of water, the chicken broth, basil, parsley, beans, and tomatoes. Bring to a boil, and add the pasta. Cook until the pasta is soft, 5 or 6 minutes.

3. Serve in bowls with shredded mozzarella on top.

· Salads ·

CAESAR SALAD
· · · · · · · · · · · · · · · · · · · ·

4 SERVINGS

Who doesn't love a Caesar salad? I use a fresh organic egg, but you can use an egg substitute if you wish.

For the dressing:
3 tablespoons extra-virgin olive oil
1 tablespoon fresh lemon juice
3 tablespoons red wine vinegar
1 egg or egg substitute
1½ to 2 teaspoons anchovy paste or 2 anchovies
1 teaspoon Worcestershire sauce
¼ teaspoon kosher salt
1 garlic clove, minced
¼ cup grated Parmesan cheese

For the salad:
2 heads romaine, washed, dried, and torn or sliced into pieces
Freshly ground black pepper
2 tablespoons freshly grated Parmesan cheese
½ cup chunky croutons

1. To make the dressing, put all the ingredients into the Cuisinart or blender and mix thoroughly until the dressing is a nice light yellow.

2. To make the salad, place the romaine into a big bowl and add in 4 tablespoons of the dressing. Coat until all the leaves are well covered. Sprinkle on the pepper and Parmesan, and top with the croutons.

MACARONI SALAD

●●●●●●●●●●●●●●●●●●●●

6 SERVINGS

Every summer barbecue needs a big bowl of macaroni salad. Pair this up with my ribs or steak sandwiches, and you'll have a great meal.

1 pound elbow macaroni
1¼ cups frozen petite peas
¼ cup diced Bermuda onion
1 cup mayonnaise
½ cup sour cream
1 teaspoon white wine vinegar
¾ teaspoon sugar
¼ teaspoon salt
Freshly ground black pepper

1. Bring a large pot of salted water to a boil. Add the macaroni and cook until al dente. Drain. Rinse with cold water and drain. Transfer the pasta to a large bowl. Cover with plastic wrap and refrigerate until cool.

2. Thaw the peas under cold running water. Add the peas and onion to the macaroni. Whisk together the mayonnaise, sour cream, vinegar, sugar, and salt, and fold into the macaroni mixture. Season with salt and pepper. Refrigerate for at least 1 hour before serving.

DARLA'S SUMMERTIME DRESSING

ABOUT ½ CUP

I love to make salad dressings—you know that. Here's one of my favorites!

2 tablespoons fresh orange juice

2 tablespoons fresh lime juice

2 teaspoons Dijon mustard

2 teaspoons honey

¼ teaspoon salt

⅛ teaspoon freshly ground black pepper

Put all the ingredients into a blender, and mix until the dressing is nice and thick. Pour it over a big bowl of mixed greens, and top with a sliced green apple.

• Potato Sides •

MASHED POTATOES WITH CHEESE

6 SERVINGS

My children just won't eat mashed potatoes without cheese.

6 medium potatoes
1¼ teaspoons kosher salt
½ cup milk
4 tablespoons butter
1 cup shredded cheddar

1. Place the potatoes in a large pot with 1 teaspoon of the salt. Add water to cover the potatoes, and bring to a boil over medium-high heat. Lower the heat to medium, and simmer 15 minutes or until the potatoes are soft and cooked through when pierced with a fork.

2. Drain the potatoes and add the milk, butter, cheese, and remaining ¼ teaspoon salt. Blend the potatoes with a potato masher until you reach the desired texture.

NOTE: The next day you can make potato pancakes from the leftover mashed potatoes. Form the potatoes into flat cakes, ½ inch high and 2 inches wide. Dip them lightly in flour, shake off any excess, and brown each side in butter over medium heat. When they're a bit crispy, serve them to the kids with applesauce for dunking. Yes, this works even with the cheesy mashed potatoes.

MY FAVORITE FRENCH FRIES

4 SERVINGS

I try to use sweet potatoes when I can disguise them, because they're rich in vitamins.

2 potatoes, peeled and cut into fries of the desired size
Vegetable oil
Salt to taste

Add ¼ inch of vegetable oil to a heavy sauté pan. Heat the oil to medium-high. When it's hot, add the potatoes (make sure you pat them dry or you might get burned) and fry them, tossing in the pan to make sure they're coated with oil and getting browned, crisp, and firm on all sides, about 10 minutes.

Drain the fries on paper towels and salt them well. Serve hot with ketchup.

· Dessert ·

HONEY BALLS (STRUFFOLI)

●●●●●●●●●●●●●●●●●●●●●●●●●●●●●●●●●

This is the Christmas dessert I spoke about earlier. My mother, aunts, cousins, and I get together before the holidays, and we make a big batch of these treats. We usually argue over the ingredients because each of the women in my mother's family has a different version of the recipe, but I've found this one to be the best. I don't know the original source, but all of my relatives are fighting over the rights to this recipe.

I don't know how many this recipe would serve, you could have a few or a bowl full. This recipe fills up a large serving dish—a nice size for a family of six to eight.

For the dough:
3 large eggs
1 tablespoon butter, softened (don't microwave, just let it sit
  for an hour before you use it; I use salted)
1 teaspoon sugar
½ teaspoon baking powder
2 cups all-purpose flour
1 cup vegetable oil

For the honey topping:
½ cup sugar
1 cup honey
Sprinkles

1. To make the dough: In a medium bowl, whisk together the eggs, butter, and 1 teaspoon of sugar until the mixture is foamy. Stir in the baking powder and flour.

2. Work the mixture with your hands until you form a soft dough. Divide it into four equal-size balls. Roll out the balls on a lightly floured surface into what I call long snakes about 1-inch thick. The kids love to do this.

3. Cut the snakes into 1-inch-long pieces. Roll the pieces into cute little balls. Let your children do this, but don't let them near the deep fryer.

4. In a deep fryer, heat the oil to 375°F. Drop the balls a handful at a time into the oil using a big slotted spoon. They will puff up and start to turn golden brown, about 2 minutes. Use the slotted spoon to remove them, and place them on paper towels to drain. Put them in a large bowl. Fry the rest of the balls.

5. To make the honey topping: In a small pot over low heat, mix the remaining ½ cup sugar and the honey. Heat, stirring constantly, until the sugar dissolves and you have a nice, loose consistency. Pour the topping over the fried balls and mix with a spoon until all the balls are coated with honey.

6. Transfer the balls to a nice dish. Pile them high into a mound and pour some sprinkles on top.

APPLE CRISP

· · · · · · · · · · · · · · · · · ·

8 SERVINGS

This is a great dessert! So easy—and yummy.

For the apple mixture:
10 small Granny Smith apples,
*   peeled and sliced*
½ cup sugar
1 cup brown sugar
Squeeze of lemon juice
1 teaspoon cinnamon
¼ teaspoon salt

For the crumb topping:
1 cup rolled oats
1 cup flour
1 cup firmly packed brown sugar
½ teaspoon baking powder
¼ teaspoon baking soda
½ cup melted butter

1. Preheat oven to 375°F.
2. To make the apple filling: In a large bowl, combine the apples, sugar, brown sugar, lemon juice, cinnamon, and salt. Place the mixture in a round 9-inch glass baking dish.
3. To make the topping mixture: In a large bowl, combine the oats, flour, brown sugar, baking powder, and baking soda. Add in the butter until the mixture is nice and crumbly.
4. Spoon the oat mixture over the apples and bake about 30 minutes or until the topping is bubbly and the apples are softened. Cool slightly and serve warm with vanilla ice cream on top.

PUMPKIN PIE

8 SERVINGS

You really do need to bake a pumpkin pie once a year—it's so much better than store-bought! To make the absolute best pie, you should use a fresh pumpkin, not the canned kind. Find a sugar pumpkin—ask the people at the farmer's market or your local produce guy. And you'll notice there's no nutmeg in my pumpkin pie recipe. I think nutmeg ruins a pumpkin pie—sorry!

Also, for Thanksgiving or any holiday, go all out and make your piecrust from scratch. You could skimp and buy premade pie crust and canned pumpkin, but I promise it won't taste as yummy. I like this crust recipe because it's easy and takes only minutes to make.

For the crust:
3 cups all-purpose flour
1½ teaspoons salt
3 tablespoons white sugar
1 cup shortening
1 egg
1 teaspoon distilled white vinegar
1 egg, beaten

For the filling:

1 sugar pumpkin, about 8 to 10 inches in diameter

1 cup packed light brown sugar

1 tablespoon cornstarch

½ teaspoon salt

1 teaspoon ground ginger

1 teaspoon ground cinnamon

⅛ teaspoon ground cloves

3 large eggs, lightly beaten

1½ cups evaporated milk

1. To prepare the pumpkin, preheat oven to 350°F and coat a baking sheet with cooking spray. Cut the pumpkin in half, scoop out all the seeds, and place it on the sheet cut-side down. Bake until the pumpkin is softened, 45 to 60 minutes. Set the pumpkin aside to cool, then scoop out the pumpkin flesh and puree it in a Cuisinart or blender.

2. To make the crust: In a large mixing bowl, combine the flour, salt, and sugar. Mix well, then cut in the shortening until the mixture resembles coarse meal.

3. In a small bowl, combine the egg, vinegar, and 4 tablespoons of water. Whisk together, then gradually add the flour mixture, stirring with a fork. Mix until the dough forms a ball. Add one more tablespoon of water if necessary.

4. Allow the dough to rest in the refrigerator for 10 minutes.

5. Roll the dough out between two large pieces of plastic wrap. Once you have a circle about 11 inches wide, drape it over a round 9-inch greased pie dish. I actually like to use a big 12-inch pie dish that I have and make a more shallow pie (this I bake 10 minutes less). Gently peel off the bottom side of the plastic wrap and press the dough down into the bottom, making sure the dough touches all the bottom surfaces. Pinch

the edges around the perimeter of the dish to make a nice edge to your pie.

6. To make the pumpkin filling: In a large bowl, combine 1½ cups of the pumpkin puree and the rest of the filling ingredients. Mix well.

7. Brush 1 beaten egg over the crust for a nice, glossy professional look. Pour the pumpkin mixture into the crust.

8. Bake at 350°F for 40 minutes or until firm.

NOTE: If you want to get really fancy, you could cut leaf shapes from the crust and place them on top of the pie filling. Make sure you brush the leaves with egg before baking.

S'MORES

4 SERVINGS, OR IN MY HOUSE, 2

S'mores are a summer campfire staple, but if you have a fireplace, it's great to use long skewers and roast marshmallows in the winter, too! We've even made them in the kitchen over a candle.

8 marshmallows
1 chocolate bar, broken into 8 pieces
4 graham crackers broken in half to make 8 pieces

Roast the marshmallows on long skewers or even a long fork, and place each one with a piece of chocolate between 2 graham crackers.

· When Company Comes . . . ·

HOT ARTICHOKE DIP

8 SERVINGS

This is delicious served hot with Ritz crackers.

2 cans water-packed artichokes, drained and quartered
1 cup mayonnaise
1 cup grated Parmesan cheese
1 package (8 ounces) shredded mozzarella
Pinch each of garlic salt, onion salt, salt, and pepper

Preheat oven to 350°F. Mix all the ingredients in a 1-quart casserole dish.
Bake 30 minutes or until hot and bubbling.

MEXICAN LAYER DIP

8 SERVINGS

This is my favorite. I love to serve it on a big platter surrounded by blue tortilla chips. And don't forget the margaritas—there are so many great drink mixes out there, and you just need to add tequila. I am a huge fan of Mike's Hard products, especially the cranberry lemonade—just serve it with ice in pretty glasses. It's a refreshing cocktail and no work at all.

For the beans:
2 tablespoons olive oil
1 small onion, chopped
3 garlic cloves, chopped
1 25-ounce can black beans, drained
1 tablespoon Adobo seasoning

For the guacamole:
2 avocados, peeled and mashed with fork
Juice of one small lime
1 small ripe tomato, diced
1 tablespoon chopped fresh cilantro
½ teaspoon salt

3 tablespoons sour cream
½ cup shredded Mexican cheese
1 small tomato, diced
2 scallions, chopped

1. To make the beans: In a large sauté pan, heat the olive oil over medium heat. Add the onion and garlic, and sauté until softened, about 5 minutes. Add the beans and Adobo and cook 5 minutes. Puree the bean mixture in a Cuisinart or blender for 20 seconds and pour it onto a big plate.

2. To make the guacamole: In a medium bowl, mix the ingredients together. Pour the guacamole over the beans, leaving an edge of beans around the outside.

3. Top the guacamole with the sour cream, cheese, diced tomato, and scallion. Surround with blue tortilla chips.

· STEP 7 ·

Keep Your Girlfriends

Don't be a bitch

Make new friends

Mommy cliques

Get involved in your community

Find a couple to hang with

Entertain

Get out of the house

I've been sitting here thinking for a few minutes about how I should write this step. I think it's a very important step, and I want to make sure you don't take it the wrong way . . . so, here it goes . . .

Your husband should not be your best friend. He's your husband, and obviously you should have a very deep bond with him, but you absolutely must have another outlet in your life. You'll never be a happy housewife if you wrap your identity entirely around your husband and children.

I'm very lucky in that I have many great women in my life. I have my girlfriends from grammar school, college, work, the old neighborhood, and the new neighborhood. I collect friends, and I always have. I love my girls, and I know I could call any one of them in a pinch and they would be there for me (except Jill—if she had a tennis match she would leave me flat; and Gina, who once left me, my baby, and her baby, who was with me at the time, out in a snowstorm for an hour when my car broke down while she closed a business deal). It's your best girlfriends who will be there for you throughout the years.

If I didn't have my girlfriends when my babies were small, I would have gone over the edge for sure. When I was depressed, lonely, or feeling sorry for myself, it was the other moms who held me up above the water.

To be honest, I rejected these moms at first. They were living in the house next door, across the street, in my town, in my community, and I thought I was too good for them. They, of course, were just housewives, and I dreaded the idea of becoming one of them. So at first I stayed away. I kept to myself on the playground. But new mommyhood is lonely, and after a while you become desperate to meet other moms. Slowly, I allowed myself to let my guard down. I learned that these women were just like me. These women were smart, successful, beautiful, strong, and more in control of their lives than I was. They became my heroes. They continue to be my strongest support system. And while, as you know, I adore my husband, it's my girls who pull me through the hardest days. It's the women in your life, the warrior mothers I call them, who you'll be able to depend on when you're depressed, fighting with your husband, losing your patience, and about to snap.

Last spring, my friend Gina called me up about 11:00 P.M. and said, "Darla . . . I'm in so much pain . . . help me." I asked her where she was, and guess what? She was calling me from her bedroom on the second floor of her house. She was up there with excruciating abdominal pain, and her husband Paul (whom I adore, but he's a man, let's face it) was downstairs in the family room watching TV. I walked into the house to find him flipping through channels in a man-stupor. I said, "Paul, Gina just called me from your bedroom. Do you know she's up there dying of pain?" He just looked dumbfounded. I went upstairs, and when I saw her I knew she had to go to the emergency room. I took her to the hospital, and a few hours later she had her appendix removed. Don't hate Paul; he's a good guy. He just isn't a woman.

This is why we have to stick together. We know the pain of childbirth, the difficulty of trying to juggle it all. On the nights when you're at your wit's end and you think you're the only mother in the world who cannot do the baby thing, it's your girls who will pull you through. If I were sick, in a bind, who would I turn to? My girls.

Our lives change dramatically after we stay home to be with our babies. Our childless career-girl friends drop us as if we have cooties, so we're left to survive the new mommy hell on our own. It really is a nightmare.

I think it's fun to share your life with your girls. Especially if your husband works a lot, like mine, hanging with another mom and her baby helps the time pass a lot faster. I used to host afternoon get-togethers at my house. I would invite about ten moms and their babies. You could start something like this and switch houses each week. You could go on the Internet and find mommy groups in your area—check out www.mommy-match.com and www.matchingmoms.com.

Let's face it, we're all growing older. Personally, I'm not taking it well. I always wanted to be thirty-five; it's the forty thing I'm getting worried about. I'm sure it's better than the alternative. We're all worried about the big C word. It could be any one of us, any time—cancer could be right around the corner. I'm terrified. I just want to be there for my children. I want to live.

When the Terri Schiavo case was in the news, it really made me really think. If I were in the hospital, very ill, who would be there for me? How long would my husband be there for me? How long would my girlfriends be there for me? Who would pluck the hairs from my chin? Who would make sure my diaper was changed? Who would make decisions for me if I couldn't? I decided that I needed to make some big choices. And while I love my husband and I know he loves me, the Schiavo story made me wonder who I should list as my guardian in my living will, my husband or my best friends? What would happen to me when my husband wanted to remarry? What would happen to my children? It's depressing to even think about it, but I must admit I'm scared.

Lucy is a best friend and blood sister, literally . . . I donated my blood to her when she had an operation in case she needed a transfusion. Now that's an example of why you need to keep your girlfriends, especially the ones with the same blood type. Anyway, we were in tears recently when we both wondered who we would entrust our children to if we died. Lucy said she would love for me to raise her children, and I said I would trust that she would love mine as her own. You know you're very lucky to find real friendships that last through the years. Lu and I went to graduate school together, have worked together, have had some big blowout arguments, and have shared our darkest secrets that we will take to the grave. We both have big mouths, and we're both a little crazy sometimes, but in the end she knows I would give her a kidney, and I know she would do the same for me. But I'm equally sure she would never loan me her Prada bag.

So do keep those close ties with your girlfriends. They'll be the ones plucking the hair from your chin when you're lying in the hospital. They're the ones who will tell you your roots are too dark. They'll pull the brownie out of your mouth when you're dieting and shove that brownie back in when you're having a meltdown.

I know I'm not alone in this thought. My girlfriends and I can stay up for hours talking about our fears. We can be hypochondriacs together. We can moan, whine, do all the girl things that we love to do—those deep, morbid conversations that your husband just doesn't want to hear. So don't bother your husband with it—call your girlfriends!

To be a happy housewife, you just have to have girlfriends. True friendships, not the backstabbing, steal-your-husband kind of friend. I have to say that I would really be afraid if I were living on Wisteria Lane. Can those women really trust each other? Would Gabriella try to steal your husband?

Don't Be a Bitch

It's funny how so many women spend so much time gossiping about other women. It's true. I think for a lot of housewives, their number one pastime is bitching about what other women are doing. "Look what she's wearing . . . Who does she think she is?" Yadda, yadda.

I know women whom I have pretty much dumped from my life because they spend most of their time talking about other women. One woman would constantly speak ill about her own best friend and make fun of her weight behind her back. One day I walked in on this woman saying something negative about my own baby, and that was it for me. She knows who she is. If she's reading this today, she should feel guilty. Shame on her. Shame on so many of us who have judged our sisters for so many trivial things.

I've heard mommies bitching to each other at the coffeehouse about so-and-so and how she did this or that. I've heard women come out of church bitching about what so-and-so was wearing. I think the reason a lot of women do this bitchy backstabbing thing is that they're insecure and talk bad about other women to make themselves feel better. I think it only makes them look bad. If you have nothing good to say, keep your mouth shut!

Hey, don't get me wrong. I have a lot of things to say. I'm the first one to tell off the teller at the bank when she treats me poorly. I'm the first one to send my food back if it's not prepared correctly. I'm the first one to open my mouth on a lot of occasions!

But I have two rules that I think are important to follow. First, I don't say anything to anyone that I don't intend to be repeated; I assume that whatever I say will get around. And second, I don't say anything behind someone's back that I wouldn't say to her face.

I recently went to a birthday party with my four-year-old daughter. When we came into the room, I saw twenty preschool children running around screaming and a Rottweiler dog walking around.

"Whose dog is this?" I asked. "The owner of the facility," I was told. But the owner was nowhere to be found. Who would call the dog off if he clamped down on one of these little necks? "Oh, no," I said. "The dog must be removed."

The women in the room all looked at me like I had a lot of nerve. Who did I think I was? Sorry, ladies, but my beautiful daughter is not going to get chewed up by this dog. I have to ask, though, what was this mother thinking? After seeing a few nasty looks coming my way, I asked the moms I knew, "Am I wrong?"

One of the women said to me, "Well, it's not what you said, it's how you said it."

I told her, "I was trying purposefully to be bitchy, because I was angry." I ask you, is it not better to be straightforward?

If you ask my circle of best girlfriends, they will all tell you that Darla is a straight shooter. She never gossips and doesn't talk about her friends. She's one to keep a secret to her death and one who knows when to keep her mouth shut. But if her mouth opens, watch out. You must have done something really stupid to get me to say something. And if that's the case, you won't hear it secondhand from someone else. You'll hear it from me.

I was upset by something one of my girlfriends said to me last year. I let it brew for a day or so, but I didn't call around to all of our friends to talk about it. I called her. I told her how I felt. I wrote her a letter. We talked it out. You know what? We're closer than ever before.

I know a lot of women who just feel badly deep down inside. They're dealing with some type of heartache, some issue, some pain. But don't let this come out in the form of criticism of other women. We moms are truly our own best support system. We need each other. Let's all stop judging each other.

Sometimes women get competitive with each other—who has more, who has less. Frankly, there will always be another mom who looks better than you and another mom who looks worse—so why bother with the comparisons?

We all have problems. One woman wishes her marriage were better, one wants to lose weight, one is having financial problems, one has a kid who's doing badly in school. We all have something going on. There's no reason to try so hard to impress your sisters. Just be you. Be happy. Talk to other moms. Let them know who you are. Accept these women for who they are and for all the beauty they have inside.

One of my neighbors once said to me, "I'm a very private person. I don't need to talk to everyone and be friends with all my neighbors." I find that to be a very sad statement, but maybe that's just me. I want to know everyone, to meet women all over the place, to hear about their lives, to share our lives together, to be open, friendly, and accepting. I know a woman who has lived in her neighborhood for thirty years, and yet she has not one lady to coffee klatch with, not one girlfriend to run to the store with, not one neighbor she could call if she were half dead on the floor. This woman shut herself off years ago, and I find this very sad.

Not having other mommies in your life, not having girlfriends to hang with, not having true friends whom you know you could count on, not having trust in your circle of girls, not having these women to laugh with—*that* would make me desperate.

So if you want to be a happy housewife, stop gossiping about your girls, open yourself up to new friendships, be nice, make new girlfriends, keep them in your life, and please don't be a bitch.

I wish we could all stop the whining, the complaining, the cliques, the bitterness. I wish we could all be great girlfriends. I wish we could all realize how lucky each one of us is and that we all have much to bring to the table. We're all the same. We're moms. We all want the best for our children. We all want a safe, clean world for them to grow up in. Let's join together and demand our rights as women. The right to good health care. The right to great friendships. The right to real intimacy. The right to grow old gracefully.

The right to have great sex. The right to be beautiful, no matter what size skirt we wear. Most important, I believe, is our right to be free. Thank God every day of your life that you're free to be the woman that you are.

Make New Friends

Being a new mom is one of the loneliest experiences—at least for me it was. I felt as if it were just me and Connor, and no one in the world cared about us. I know it sounds crazy, considering I had family and friends who lived right up the road, but that's how I felt—all alone.

As you know, I at first rejected the idea of being one of these housewives in suburbia, but it was those very women whom I rejected at first who saved me in the end. It was these women who helped me get through the day. It was these women who helped me in the middle of the night when my baby had a temperature of 104 and I was hysterical. It was these women who sat for me while I ran to the doctor. It was these women who were there for me, and I'm grateful.

I know it can be hard to meet new women and make real friendships. While you think it might be hard to "hook up," as I say it, other women out there are looking to hook up just as much. That's why there are so many mommy-and-me groups out there—not for the sake of the baby, but for the sake of the mommy. We're desperate to talk to other mothers, to be with other women, to have adult conversation, to get out of the house, to make new friendships.

If you're a new mother, it's easy to meet other new moms. Go to the park, join a Mingling Moms group in your town (check out www.minglingmoms.com), go hang out at the coffee shop—if you go out with a stroller, other mothers will flock to you. It's a huge pick-up scene, moms picking up other moms. Just be friendly and start conversations. It's easy to talk about baby stuff or make a playdate, and it's a good excuse. But do get out of the house with your baby or you'll go crazy. Bond with other moms, or your brain will turn to baby food.

Once you've made those bonds, you'll have someone to watch out for your children. Someone to call when you're about to lose it. Someone to go out with when you leave the children at home to play with daddy. It's good for mommy to get out for a little fun. We can still go out for cocktails, dinner, a movie, definitely shopping—and believe me, your husband doesn't want to see most of the movies you're interested in, so take your girls to the chick flick. Movie theaters now offer special movie times just for moms and their babies. Loew's Cineplex offers Reelmoms—bring your babies to the movies, it's a great idea. Now your baby can scream her head off, you can whip out your boob and nurse while you chomp on popcorn, and no one will get upset.

Mommy Cliques

It's really sad, but you see them everywhere. They're like a bunch of vultures waiting for prey, and then they spot one—an unsuspecting new mother trying to enter into their territory, whether it's at Mommy and Me, Mingling Moms, Mustermusik, or just at the park. The established mothers spot the newcomer and slowly work her over, looking for any wound that can be found to pick at. They look over what you're wearing, what your baby is wearing, the stroller you use, whether or not you're carrying a designer diaper bag, and they decide if you're worthy of talking to and if your baby is good enough for theirs to play with. And the new mommy waits alone trying to occupy herself with her baby, desperate for one of the moms to make a move. It's a huge pick-up scene. It sounds cruel, but it's true. All new mommies have been in this position. Desperate for a new friend, another woman to bond with to try to ease the hours of boredom, we join these groups not for our kids' stimulation but for ours. Each woman tries her best to pick up another cute mom for a potential long-lasting relationship. And let me tell you, it's even more denigrating than the singles scene. At least with men you know where you stand. They screw you and then you don't hear from them. Better yet, they tell you straight out they're not looking for a long-term relationship. With women it's tricky.

My girlfriend tells the best story about the crazy women in her town. All the new mommies at Mingling Moms are trying to hook up with each other. Some pair off, but mostly the group as a whole becomes friendly. My girlfriend was devastated, though, when the girl she brought into the group dumped her for a new girl she met at the group. Now those two girls are hanging at the park with their babies, and my friend is back trying to pick up a new mom.

We really never leave high school. No matter how many graduate degrees we earn, it goes out the window when we're back on the playground with our babies. The whole mommy clique thing is stronger than ever in the suburbs. I have been really studying this phenomenon, and it's a clear fashion thing. I notice that the cute, stylish moms hang out with other cute, stylish moms, and the frumpy moms hang out with the other frumpy moms. I told this to my girlfriend, and she told me months later that that statement alone got her off her bottom and to the gym. Now she has a slew of new girlfriends, and she's in the A-list mommy clique—which is stupid, I know, but it's just the way it is. So look good, don't be a bitch, and maybe you could be the new popular mom in town.

Get Involved in Your Community

Knowing your neighbors is important. It's good for your children to have people in their community watching out for them, and it's good for you to have people you know to help you out. Join a church. Become a member of the PTA. Get on the beautification committee. Be part of your community. Caring about the town you live in and knowing the people in the area can bring you an enormous amount of peace and sense of safety.

I love knowing the shopkeepers in my town. When I go to the butcher, he knows me by name. When my children go to the park, there are always other moms there that we know. It's a huge support system that all of us moms need. Being able to call one of my girlfriends in a pinch is great. Having neighbors you can count on last-minute can make your life so much easier.

Go out of your way to make contact. Say hello. Talk to the people you see. These are the people in your community, so get to know them.

Find a Couple to Hang With

When you're out there making new mommy friends, try to pick a mom who has a hubby you also like. This is very important. If you don't like her husband, you're going to have a hard time keeping the friendship alive. I have one friend who knows that I'm not too thrilled with her hubby, but it's okay because she's not thrilled with him either. I think he's a cheap, emotionally abusive bastard and she's too good for him, but she stays with him for now because she has young children to support. She knows she has my full support, love, friendship, and encouragement, and hopefully one day her husband will evolve into the nice guy we're trying to create, but for now we bite our tongues, look the other way, and let him make a jackass out of himself.

Anyway, it's sad for her that none of her friends wants to hang out with them as a couple, although she manages to joke about it. We get together during the day—just us girls—and we have a lot of fun.

But it's great when you can find a playmate for your hubby too. Now you can go out on a double date. Let's face it, girls, most men just don't make friends on their own. They have the same friends they had in high school and college, and once they get married most of those relationships dwindle down. It's up to you to find a mom with a hubby who can play with your hubby. This works out especially well if you all end up traveling together. The husbands could go play golf while the women shop (and make sure you get a great resort that has child care!).

Yes, some things are even more fun when you're sharing the time with another couple. Bill and I go out to dinner with our friends, we've vacationed with them, and we've had a lot of laughs. Paul, I know you would be devastated if I didn't talk about you in this book, so I'll mention the time we were on that spinning teacup ride in Florida. Both families went down to Disney World together, and I've never laughed as hard as I did that night when Paul and I kept spinning that teacup.

Over the years my best friends' husbands have become some of my husband's best friends. We ski together, barbecue together, go out on the weekends together, and it's all a lot of fun.

If your husband is one of those guys who doesn't want to meet new people, or says he doesn't want to hang with your friend's husband, talk him into trying it. I'll bet he has a good time.

No matter how great your marriage is, no matter how hot your sex life is, just being the two of you will get pretty boring if you never bring other couples into your life. Oh, and don't read into that . . . I'm not talking about the bedroom. I'm just saying that it's fun to go out as couples. Just make sure you have a lot in common. I have friends who don't drink alcohol; Bill and I won't go on vacation with them because we want to have cocktails and get tipsy, and let's face it, it's no fun to be with sober people when you have a load on. Bill and I have friends who love to lie on the beach, but we like to sightsee all day, so we won't be vacationing with them either.

We have dinner with friends who love food as much as we do. We ski with our skiing friends. We drink with our drinking buddies. And we stay home with our homebody friends. We're lucky that we know so many great couples. But hey, Bill and I are pretty great, and everyone wants to be friends with us, too.

If you open yourselves up, you might meet some really terrific people.

Entertain

Ever since I was a little girl I've had a habit of inviting every person I meet over to my house. My girlfriend Cathy, whom I have known forever, jokes about how on the first day I met her in the fourth grade I invited her to my birthday party. I'm still that way. All my girls have been calling me lately and accusing me of changing, because I haven't had one of my Darla shindigs in a very long time, since we moved into this house almost a year ago, I think. I've been so busy writing this book that I've let it completely take over my life. So, as soon as I'm done I'll throw a huge party—adults only, of course—and we'll all have a great time.

I say adults only because mommies and daddies need to get out and have some fun, too. The kids always go to birthday parties, Halloween parties, and school dances, and what do we get to do? I like to throw great parties for the moms and dads to dance, drink, and have fun. My sister-in-law once got really mad because I said there were no children allowed at my husband's fortieth birthday party. We were going to a fancy restaurant in Manhattan, taking a limo into the city, and we wanted to booze it up and have fun without having to watch what we did or said because a child was there. I think it's crucial for parents to have some fun too. If you never go out without your children—not even to dinner and a movie—it's a little ridiculous. As I said earlier, you have to get out with your husband and have alone time if you want your marriage to thrive. Plus, as a woman, you need to have some time away from your children.

If you have young babies and are not ready to part—yes, I know what that's like— then have smaller gatherings with one or two couples who have young children. Face facts, girls, no childless woman or couple wants to hang out with you and your babies. If you don't have a baby, being around someone else's baby for more than a short time is just annoying. We all know it. And once our children are getting older, it's hard to make plans with someone who has a baby because we're worried your baby will hold us back. Sorry, but it's true.

I'm finally in the almost-free mode. This winter, skiing was fabulous because Connor and Hannah were in ski school all day learning the sport with instructors and Bill and I were up on the mountain. When we go skiing we usually go with our best friends Sean and Jill, because they have children the same age as ours so we're all on the same schedule. If a baby were thrown into that mix, it would not be good. Sorry again.

But for those of you who have babies, make sure you hook up with a couple who has a baby, too. You can invite them over, have a nice dinner while the babies sleep or play together, and you'll have a lot of fun.

The important thing is that we value all our friends, and we always say that we're very lucky to have so many great people in our life.

Open yourselves up to meeting new couples and having some laughs together.

Get Out of the House

I was recently at a fashion show that our school threw to raise money for the PTA, and I suggested that next time they have a fund-raiser they do a blackjack night so the husbands would want to come, too. The women said that they made the fashion show for the moms only, because the women wanted to have something just for themselves so they could get out of the house. I couldn't believe that these women needed an excuse to get out of the house. Why was that? I wondered.

Then I realized that many moms feel guilty about leaving their kids. They feel as if they're abandoning them, as if some horrible thing will happen to their children if they're not there. I know, I felt that way, too. When Connor was a newborn, I wouldn't even go to the store without him. I wouldn't leave him with my mother, my husband, no one. I wore him on my body and slept with him. (I'm still sleeping with him, only now I want him out of the bed and he won't go.) I was obsessed with him, and I didn't leave the house without him until he was six months old. Even then, it was just for a quick hour to get my hair cut, as I recall. But what I was doing was isolating myself, and I'm convinced that that's why I started feeling desperate. When you don't allow yourself any pleasure or freedom, you become crazier than you were before you had the baby. Then you really become a nag to your husband, and soon you're drifting off into a world of your own.

You cannot allow this to happen. You just have to get out of the house and meet other mommies. You have to talk like an adult. You have to keep some of your identity. You have to have fun. You have to do all these things if you want to be happy.

We're all in the same boat. We're all trying to hold on to that fountain of youth. We're all trying to save our marriages. We're all trying to raise good kids. We're all trying to do the best we can, so let's all try to help each other. Cut the immature, competitive, cliquish crap and start supporting each other. Be nice. Don't be a bitch. Let's all be friends. Be a girls' girl. And whatever you do, don't steal your girlfriend's husband.

Make Time for Yourself

Do something you enjoy

Take care of mommy

Remember, your life is not over

Get in touch with your spirituality

Ah. . . . Right now, I'm sitting at my kitchen island writing this on my laptop, with a hot cup of tea at my side, and there's silence. My children are in school—Hannah for only two hours, so I don't have much time—but for this hour that I have left, I won't clean, I won't cook, I'll do only what I want to do, because it's Darla time!

Maybe it's a bit selfish. There's laundry to do. My bedroom closet is a disaster. I have a dozen calls to return. Our dog smells; I should bathe her. But I can do it all later. Right now I'm enjoying my time alone. . . . no kids, no hubby, no pressure. I need this time. Does that make me a bad homemaker, a rotten mother? Just the opposite. When I get to spend some time doing something I enjoy, something just for me, I'm a much calmer mother, a saner wife, and a happier homemaker.

You must make time each day just for yourself. This is critical in order for you to keep your sanity and not lose your patience with your children or your husband. I know many moms who run ragged all day long, cooking, cleaning, driving the kids all over town, and by the end of the day they're exhausted and the best thing they can do for themselves is to plop into bed and go to sleep.

Who says being an at-home mom means that you have to spend every waking moment playing mommy? It's just not true. To be a great mom you need to stay a clear-thinking, happy woman, and that means you need to have time for yourself, get out once in a while without the babies, and, as I said earlier, have some alone time with your hubby. You know that Bill and I have date night every week. I really look forward to it. Sometimes I'm already out there at the curb when he pulls down the block. The neighbors must wonder what I'm doing all dressed up standing at the corner, but I'm so desperate to get out that as soon as the babysitter shows up I'm out the door. I would rather wait in the street than be at home another minute. Oh, stop. You know I adore my children. But I need some time without them, and you do, too.

Last week a few of my girlfriends got together for a girls' night. All we wanted to do was to get out of the house, have a few cocktails, and eat some great food. Four of us met at Oscars, a local restaurant that I love, and we were all joking at the bar about how hard it was to get out of the house. My mother came to watch the children, but Hannah hung onto my leg and begged me not to leave. The poor child . . . I basically pushed her off of me. I'm sure she'll need therapy for that one. But you know what that's like. That separation anxiety is enough to make a mommy crazy. The funny thing was that as quickly as I could pull out of my driveway was as quickly as I felt as if I should pull back in. We all torture ourselves over this mommy guilt, as if we're horrible women to want to get out.

After a couple of margaritas and some quesadillas, the cell phones started ringing. One husband couldn't find the purple Barbie nightgown, one baby-sitter needed to leave, one child developed a fever, and my daughter never stopped crying. We laughed, and we left.

It didn't matter, though. By the time each of us got home we were in a great mood. Of course, the alcohol helped, but just getting out with the girls even for a short time was a nice pick-me-up. Many of us feel guilty leaving our children for our own enjoyment, as if we just don't deserve to have lives because we're moms. This is crazy. You have to have some fun.

I'm not saying you should start bar hopping. But it's perfectly acceptable for you to get a sitter and get out with your hubby, a girlfriend, or by yourself. Some of my most peaceful moments are spent in a mental fog wandering up and down the aisles of Costco for hours with my coffee, tasting all the samples, and buying a lot of stuff we don't need.

I know we all have obligations, but there's no reason to live under such pressure. You *can* relax and still get it all done. It's a state of mind.

If you're anxious or overwhelmed, it will make you more stressed out than you need to be. You'll get it all done. Now that you know how to stay organized, on schedule, now that you look better and are having a closer relationship with your husband, taking care of mommy is the next thing you need to do.

So, let's sit back for a minute. Breathe. Meditate for a few minutes. Go ahead, I'll wait. . . .

Okay, let's begin. This is what I want you to do. In the morning after you send everyone out the door, before you get on with your day, I want you to lie on the bed (after you've made it, of course) for a few moments and just thank God for all the blessings in your life. Thank yourself for being so great, pray for your family, and simply breathe deeply for a few minutes.

If you have babies and small children at home, include them in this ritual. Lie on your bed with your baby, stare at her, smell her, just have a few peaceful moments just you and your baby, before you begin your hectic day. If you have a toddler, this is a great time to teach him calmness. Yes, even a two-year-old enjoys lying with mommy for special quiet time. Rub your baby's back, tickle her feet, cuddle together, and talk to her about the new day, the new adventures ahead, what you'll do together, and what you expect of her. Every morning when I wake Connor up, I remind him how lucky he is to have this new day, that it's a gift from God, that he has to make the best of it, and that I expect him to be a nice, kind boy. It's never too early to teach your children to appreciate their lives.

That's the key here—appreciate your life. Take time to enjoy it. Being a mom doesn't mean you have to lose yourself to your housework, errands, or taking care of everyone else. Take care of Mommy, too. Bond with yourself. Know who you are. Be the woman you always wanted to be. Stay in touch with yourself. Don't feel guilty about it. You deserve it.

You know that I do my housework a few hours each morning so I make sure that my afternoons are free. I take time to get together with a girlfriend, go shopping, write, garden, surf the Internet, or read, cozied up in my favorite chair with a hot cup of tea. I always give myself at least one hour to rejuvenate, because we all know right after dinner is the witching hour with the children. Even when Connor and Hannah were babies, I would put them in the playpen or swing or on the floor right next to me with some blocks for them, and I would read magazines (I'm a magazine addict) and drink green tea with honey. This quiet time would help me feel relaxed and ready to be mommy again. If I needed to leave the house for mommy-time, such as having my hair highlighted (yes, mom, you must keep up your hair or you'll feel terrible), my friends and I would do a mom-swap: you watch my kid, I'll watch yours. Dana and I did this regularly, and it was great because I knew my babies were having fun and being well cared for, and I was able to get to the salon or gym.

And ladies, I advise you to leave the baby with your girlfriend or your mother instead of your husband. One day while I was getting highlights—and I'm not a blonde, so you know I'm there for a good two hours working on these roots—Bill must have called me five times: "Where's the formula, where's the binkie, how long do I have to burp her, she just threw up, Connor is missing, oh, I found him hiding in the laundry room." I was so embarrassed. Ultimately, with my hair up in foils, I had to drive home to show him where Connor's jersey was because he had peewee baseball and, of course, Bill couldn't find the jersey, which was exactly where I told him it was, in the top drawer of Connor's dresser. You get the idea, girls? I would have had a very peaceful afternoon if my mother or Dana had taken care of the kids. They would have improvised. Men are just not capable of that. Sorry, guys.

But now that the children are older, I have the life. Bill can actually handle being alone with them for a few hours. They're pretty self-sufficient, and everything runs very smoothly. I recently went for a touch-up, and there were no calls. I'm free. Well, almost.

I don't know what I'm going to do with myself in September when Hannah is in full-time kindergarten. Have another baby? Work part time? I don't know. I have to be here in the morning to get the kids off to school, and home again for them in the afternoon. What could I do in those hours? This is a dilemma shared by many women. Maybe I'll start a work-share program for moms. That would be nice. Maybe I'll catch up on all the decorating I want to do around the house. Maybe I'll take a cooking class. Maybe I'll just take some time for myself. Really, I've been working around the clock since Connor was born seven years ago. What job, you ask? Motherhood . . . it's a full-time position. Maybe it will be nice to have the day to myself for a while. It will feel really good.

Do Something You Enjoy

I know there's something you really enjoy doing but you haven't done in a long time because you're just too busy. So what is it? Painting, dancing, singing—whatever it is, you need to do it. Go take a class. One of my girlfriends is taking singing lessons. Another girlfriend started her first tap-dance classes last year at age forty. My sister just took up belly dancing. My other friend is learning to play the piano. I'm taking tennis lessons.

Why not use your time to do something you've always wanted to do? Stop putting it off. Go for it. Don't be shy. You'll find that there are a lot of women just like you who are starting to pay some attention to themselves now that the baby thing is under control. You'll have a lot of support from these women, and you'll have a lot of fun.

When I was young I had a friend whose mother was the most miserable, nasty nag I ever met. She was unhappy about everything, talked badly about everyone, and bitched and moaned about her life, especially her husband. I couldn't stand her. She had a big house and a successful husband, and I could never figure out what she was so miserable about. Now that I'm older, though, I realize that she had just allowed herself to evolve into a lifeless housewife.

I remember her jealousy over her best friend's life and marriage. She was upset that her friend was playing tennis, and I remember her calling it juvenile that the friend was taking ballet lessons. "She's too old, for God's sake," she would say. Now I realize that my friend's mother was simply envious. She didn't have the courage to enjoy herself, and she was in a rut.

My aunt Angie always says this about herself. "Darla, I'm in a rut. I just can't get out of it." I think a lot of women get stuck in this cycle of misery, this housewife ho-hum that they just don't know how to change. I'd like to help a lot of women get out of this cycle, but I think a lot of older women are just too far gone. I think they can't turn back because they believe it's just too late. My aunt is sixty-one, and I think she has plenty of living to do, a whole world to explore, yet she has lost her desire. My mother is only fifty-seven, and she's always saying her life is over. Anytime she gets annoyed at my father, she holds her chest and screams, "Somebody shoot me and put me out of my misery." So there you have the two crazy Messina sisters—one's in a rut, and one wants someone to take her down. In reality, they both just like to complain. If they weren't bitching about something, they would have nothing to talk about.

The problem is that my mother and my aunt wrapped their entire lives, their identities, around their families. Both got married very young and were mothers by age twenty. My mother says she never wanted to do anything but to be at home with my sister and me. Now that all the children are out of the house, they feel empty.

The best I could hope for them is that they will try to do something for themselves, to find something that they enjoy. For the first time in my mother's life she's working, and she loves it. My aunt, who is afraid to leave Long Island, is finally considering going to Las Vegas on vacation. It's scary for them to change their lives. It's terrifying for most of us to change our routines. I wish I could stop every older woman and have a cup of coffee with her and just talk. I would love to hear what they have to say. I imagine they would all like to turn back the clock, to spend more time being the women they used to be. I would love to ask each of them what their dreams were when they were younger. I wish I could help reignite the spark inside them.

I would bet that most of these women would advise the moms of my generation to hold on to ourselves, to try to keep some of our own dreams alive. I think they would want us to hold on to our identities.

Hold on for a minute. I'm going to call my aunt right now and ask her this question: What advice at your age would you give a mom my age? (Which is thirty-eight, by the way.) Here's what she said: "Put time aside for yourself and do what you want to do. Make sure you don't deprive yourself. If you enjoy something, you should continue to do it even though you're a mom. Then, after the kids are gone, you still have something to fall back on."

I asked her what it was that she gave up, what her dreams were. She told me that she really had no other dreams, that she wanted to be a mom raising her children, she just wished she had taken up a hobby, kept up her friendships, and forced herself not to turn her house into her cocoon. "I think I hid out in my house. I felt secure here. I wish I'd had the courage to get out there and try new things." I asked what held her back. "Guilt," she said.

You don't have to feel guilty about spending time on yourself. You don't have to feel guilty about doing something you love. Yes, you want what is best for your family, but do not lose yourself in the hectic life of mothering. Make time for yourself. Do something you enjoy. Do something just for you. Learn from my aunt.

Take Care of Mommy

Many women, including myself, put off the really important things that we should be doing because when we have a free hour we would rather sit at home than run to the dentist or the doctor. Like me right now. I've had this pain in my neck for weeks now. . . . I should be at my doctor's but I opted for some R&R. I promise I'll go this week. I have to do this for myself, for my children. What's more important than staying healthy for our children? You need to get regular physicals, Pap smears, and mammograms. Once you're over age thirty-five, you need to start paying more attention to what is going on with your body. The American Cancer Society suggests women begin having yearly mammograms at age forty, but the Academy of Family Physicians believes you should wait until age fifty—unless breast cancer runs in your family. I had my first one at thirty-five, as you know, after I found that lump in my breast. It ended up being nothing, thank God! I found the lump when I was in the shower. Make sure you give yourself a breast exam at different times during the month, when you have your period and when you don't. To learn how, go to www.vh.org (Virtual Hospital). Please eat right and take vitamin supplements. You need extra calcium and magnesium. There's a book that I recommend called *Revitalize Your Hormones: Dr. Dale's 7 Steps to a Happier, Healthier, and Sexier You* by Theresa Dale (Hoboken, NJ: John Wiley & Sons, 2005), and I think every woman over thirty-five should read it.

Remember that part of your me-time has to be taking care of mommy. You need to think about yourself when you're meditating and listen to what your body tells you. What your gut is telling you can save your life.

When I was giving birth to Connor, he got stuck in the birth canal. He should have been delivered by C-section, but the doctor got to the hospital too late and Connor was stuck. His heart stopped beating, I was having convulsions, and what should have been an easy delivery turned into a code blue situation. Ultimately, my gynecologist had to cut through my rectum to get Connor out. Thank God, my baby was fine. However, four months later I was still in agony, and every time I went to the bathroom I would scream.

I had to have a proctologist resew me because I wasn't healing correctly. The whole thing was a nightmare. This is another reason I started spiraling into my depression.

My body was already traumatized from my delivery disaster, but I started to develop a whole array of new problems—symptoms and phantom pain that I ignored or dismissed because I was just too busy with my newborn baby and I didn't want to miss a minute of being with my son. I spent a year with Connor on my boob, refusing to leave him with anyone. I was obsessed with him and terrified of SIDS, and I neglected my own health.

Eventually, I couldn't lift my head off the pillow or step onto the bedroom floor without excruciating pain. I finally made the time to get myself to a doctor. They diagnosed me. I had Lyme disease. I had to go on antibiotics for months and months. Thank goodness, it could be cured. I think what keeps us moms from going to the doctor is our fear of hearing the worst possible news. So, we live in denial. This is dangerous.

I urge all my girls out there not to put yourself last. Please, make time for yourself, get in touch with your inner spirit, stay healthy, and stay alive.

You still have so much to do.

Remember, Your Life Is Not Over

Even though we may have left our careers or put our dreams on hold to raise our children and care for our families, it doesn't mean we have to give up our dreams. My dream since I was a teenager was to be a writer. Hopefully, someone will buy this book and my dream will come true, now that I'm pushing forty.

Of course, I'm afraid—of failing, that people won't like my book, that people won't like me. I have the same fears that you do. I'm insecure, too. But even though I'm afraid, I continue to write. Why? Because I love it, it's therapeutic, I have a message, and I want to help women out there realize that being a housewife doesn't mean it's all over. It's really just the beginning. So I'm going to force myself to forge ahead and finish this book. If I don't do it, it will be the fourth time I've written something and given up. I've had a lot of ideas and I've started writing books before. Life always gets in the way, and the book goes under the bed and is forgotten. This time, however, I'm going to stick with it. It's time for me to step up for myself and do something just for me.

I'll tell you how I motivated myself to finally go through with this. I knew I wanted to write this book, but I was scared to go through with it. As my aunt said, it's easier to hide out in your house. If I actually committed myself to doing this, then I would be fulfilling my dream, living it, and that is terrifying. Then one day I was driving down the road with the radio up while the children and I were singing and a rap song came on. I wanted to change it, but my son said, "Leave it on, Mom," so I did and I heard these words:

"If you had one shot, or one opportunity to seize everything you ever wanted—one moment, would you capture it or just let it slip?"

The singer (who I now know is Eminem, and the song is "Lose Yourself") affected me in such a way that his words were meant for me to hear at that very minute. So Eminem, I love you. I'm a huge fan now.

As crazy as it sounds, it was a rapper who got my butt in gear. It was a day driving my children to play dates when I realized it was time for me to make my move. So, like the song says, I decided in that moment that I was going to seize the opportunity. When I got home I was pumped up. I sent my work out, and I got a book deal sooner than I expected. My dream was coming true, and there was no turning back.

When you have a feeling deep inside, a dream about what you want to do, go for it. Don't think your life is over, not even for a minute. Think about all your experiences so far. Think about the woman you are. Think about how strong you are and how you could still be whatever you dreamed you'd be. Being a mom is a dream come true, and taking care of your family is your job, but there's more out there for you if you want it.

Think about the freedom being at home allows you to follow your dreams. When I think about my television career and how I missed out on so many opportunities, I realize that it was never my dream to be a producer—it just happened. I think a lot of women out there are in jobs for the money, for the status, or simply because it came their way, but I doubt they're truly living their dreams.

It may be presumptuous for me to say, but by now you know I'm a bit nervy. I think most women, if asked, would say that their dream would be to spend more time with their family, not more time in the office. I know that women spend years dreaming of their wedding, dreaming of having babies, dreaming of being a mom, dreaming of being happy. Yes! Your life is a dream. How great is that?

For those of us lucky enough to be able to be home with our families, we have the true luxury of doing something really great for ourselves, our families, and society.

One of my dreams, besides writing this book, is to help women understand that being a housewife is an opportunity—an opportunity to fulfill your dreams and the dreams of your children. Living a full, happy, healthy life is a dream come true.

I have other dreams. I want to be a chef, I want to travel the world, I want to watch my children get married, I want to retire with my husband and live on the coast of Nova Scotia. Just like you, I have a lot of dreams. Having the courage to live your dreams is the hard part.

You might get rejected. It might be a long shot. When I sent out my story pitch, I was terrified. I thought for sure it would be sent back with a "Sorry, no thanks" note. Lucy auditioned last week for a television show. We're still waiting to hear if she got the part. My cousin, who is terrified to fly, just went to Africa because her dream was to go on a real safari.

Dreaming is easy, but going for it is terrifying.

So, girls, you have the rest of your lives ahead of you. What are you going to do? You are smart, beautiful women who need to live life to its fullest. You are mothers, you are warriors. The world is out there, and if there's a dream in your heart, something that you love, a need to do something, then you should go for it. It's not over for you—it's just the beginning.

I said it earlier, and I'll say it a million times, these are the best years of our lives. Rejoice, be proud, feel great, live healthfully, and never forget who you are.

A lot of women lose themselves somewhere along the way. They give up their dreams. You don't have to do that. Use your mommy-time to paint, volunteer, play golf, whatever it is that you enjoy. Take a class, finish your degree, learn how to ski—just go ahead and start doing something that you love.

It's not too late. It's not over.

Remember, we're hot mamas, with men who love us, and we're just getting started. We're going to get our acts together, start supporting each other, step up to the microphone, and make sure our voices are heard. The way I see it, we happy housewives have it all going on, and this is just the beginning.

Get in Touch with Your Spirituality

Every morning I thank God that I woke up. Just having a new day is pretty amazing to me, and I'm grateful. I take a few moments to meditate each morning, and each day I ask for wisdom. I pray that I'll be patient with my children that day. I pray to be a nicer person, a better friend, a supportive wife. I pray for us all. I find these moments very relaxing. It also keeps me in touch with my spirit. I feel refreshed, and then I continue with my day.

If you can take a few minutes every day to meditate, you'll be amazed at how wonderful you feel. Breathe deeply and forget about everything. Try to get in touch with your own spirituality. Try to reach inside yourself into your soul. Try hard to understand yourself, why you're here and what you're meant to do.

I believe that we're all part of something bigger, much bigger. I believe there's a plan for us all. I try my best every day to push myself a little further, to be the woman I was meant to be, whoever she is. I sometimes feel as if I'm blind, walking along a path, and I have no idea where I'm going. I think a lot of us feel this way. I think a lot of women bury themselves in nonsense that doesn't matter because they have not been able to reach deep within themselves to find peace.

These women are empty. Most of this society is empty, consumed with greed and competition, in a rat race to the top, never looking back and leaving loved ones behind. All this effort to keep up with the Joneses has destroyed us all. It all doesn't matter. When you're on your deathbed, will you be wearing those six-hundred dollar Gucci mules?

This really makes me crazy. Women spending all their husband's money on designer clothes, trying to act like hotshots in expensive cars they can't afford, and trying to outdo each other—it's all craziness. It's all stupid. These are your girls. These are your sisters. Why are you trying to one-up them? Why can't you be happy for them? Truly happy? Are we that insecure? Is that the woman you want to be?

I wish all the best for you. I want all of us housewives to look beautiful; to live long, happy lives; to lift each other up; to help raise our children together; to remember that one day not too far away, we just might be playing canasta together in the old-age home with our wrinkled faces, droopy implants, saggy asses, and fake teeth. In the long run, it's not the Prada or Coach bag that's going to matter. What is going to matter is what kind of woman you were. What kind of friend you were. What kind of mother you were. You still have time to change. It's not over.

Reach deep inside of you and find out who you are. Be a good neighbor. Teach your children about compassion. Show them by example. Give them the best gift of all: the gift of self-awareness. Teach them about consequence and forgiveness. Teach them about acceptance. Help them grow up to be people full of love, not jealousy. Tell them about those less fortunate. Let them know at a very young age how lucky they are to have life. Teach them to appreciate everything. Our children have so much. It's important that we encourage them to appreciate all the little things in life and how beautiful they really are. Ice cream cones with sprinkles, four-leaf clovers, finger painting, and all the fun things that go with childhood. Connor has a computer, a Game Boy, a Play Station, and about fifty game cartridges to go with these games. These things cost hundreds of dollars, so how can I get him to appreciate the little things? I talk about it with him and point them out every single day. I want him to know how lucky he is. How lucky we all are.

Each night when we lie in bed (yes, they're both still in my bed . . . I have been trying to get them out, I need the *Nanny 911* ladies), we pray together. We ask God to watch over the poor, the sick, the children all over the world.

I hope I'm teaching my children to live deep lives. To not get caught up in all this greed, this what-about-me-and-screw-everyone-else attitude. I want them to care about the world. I want them to be secure in who they are. I want them to be stronger than I am. I want them to have more courage than I do.

On a website that I like, www.spiritualityhealth.com, I read this beautiful quote from Mother Teresa: "If we have no peace it is because we have forgotten that we belong to each other."

I think about that often. It's late now and I'm tired. I have to go to bed. Looking back on this day I would say that I screamed way too much at the children. I lost my patience with Connor and gave him a smack on the behind. I was rude to my best friend, and I wish I could start the day over. I promise to do a better job at life tomorrow.

The best I can do right now is to be better myself. Each day I try harder. I pray and I meditate. I'm trying to know myself, to get in touch with my spirituality and not get caught up in the stupid stuff. I'm trying to understand why I'm here, what I was meant to do. I search my soul every day. It's the best that I can do for now.

I said in the beginning of this book that I have wisdom. I say that in jest. I can only pray that one day that is true. I do know that I'm wiser than I was ten years ago, and I can only hope that ten years from now I'll be wiser still. This is a learning experience. Every day, I try to learn more (some of my favorite books and websites are listed in the Resources section). Join me. Open your ears, your eyes, your heart, and your soul.

Don't Take It All So Seriously

Laugh it off

Scream!

It's okay to admit some days really do suck

Try to accept the things you can't change

Forgive

Remember you're strong, you can be great at this

If you take your life too seriously, you'll definitely end up a desperate housewife. It's not worth it to worry about every little detail because most of the time it doesn't matter. I have girlfriends who agonize for days over every little decision. Karen has been trying to pick out a new front door for her house for at least a year now. Angela drives herself crazy over every tiny aspect of any project she takes on, from making chocolate-covered pretzels to finding matching outfits for her children. Gina won't even allow herself to enjoy her own dinner parties; in the middle of the get-together, while her guests are drinking, talking, and enjoying themselves, she's off vacuuming the kitchen floor or wiping down the counters. Andrea cleans her house before the cleaning lady comes. Jill doesn't like to have people over because she doesn't want her house to get dirty. Bill, my husband, is such an overorganizer that he has an office that's completely off limits to me. He goes crazy if any of his paperwork is not perfectly aligned.

I think all of this is a bit over the top. While you've heard me suggest over and over that I want all housewives to get their acts together, I certainly do not want anyone out there to spend too much time worrying about things that really don't matter.

Maybe I'm too laid back. I've sat here writing for hours while I can see that there are fingerprints all over my refrigerator. I know I should wipe it down, but I just did it this morning, and the kids are coming home soon, and they're going to be looking in the fridge for snacks, and it's going to get all gunked-up again, so why waste my time? Bill says my desk has always looked like a disaster zone. I'm looking at it right now, and yes, it's covered with about thirty magazines, a pile of school papers, Connor's projects that need to be completed, and, of course, coupons. But who cares? The rest of the house is in order, the beds are made, the bathrooms are clean, and you know what? Everything is not going to be perfect at the same time every minute of my life. I'm not going to take every little detail seriously.

I really don't care that much about my front door. In fact, I bought all my wallpaper for my house in half an hour on the Internet without ever seeing it in person. It now looks gorgeous on the walls. When I went shopping for my wedding gown, I chose the first one I tried on. It was beautiful, and I was fine with it. I bought this house after looking at it once for about five minutes. Yes, I know I'm completely opposite of most people, but I just cannot waste my time thinking about things that really don't matter to me. What mattered to me was that my children lived on a cul-de-sac with other kids, that we had a good school district, and that we had a pool. I saw that the house had those things, so I didn't worry about anything else, which was stupid, because I didn't learn until we moved in that it didn't have a dishwasher, built-in barbecue, or an oil burner that worked properly.

Anyway, I got what was important to me, and the small things I could fix.

A friend recently asked me, "What floats your boat? An expensive car, diamonds, really expensive champagne?"

I said no to all of those things. What floats my boat is eating out at great restaurants and traveling. I asked my husband this question the other night on our date at my favorite restaurant in New York City, Bobby Flay's Mesa Grill. His answer? "Being with you." You see why I love him. But this is why we're together. We love food, vacations, and

· STEP 9 ·

our family. And neither of us waste any time worrying about our vacations either; I usually book them just days in advance. I don't worry about every little detail—I figure whatever it is we will have fun. Last year, I was really bored and went on the Internet and found a really cheap last-minute trip to Disney World. I called Bill and said, "I'll pick you up in two hours. We're flying to Florida." It was totally last minute, and it was a blast. The children loved rush-packing a few things, and not having too much time to think about it made it really exciting for them.

My friends make fun of me because they say I'm way too spontaneous. But it's not that I'm superspontaneous; it's just that I don't want to waste a lot of my time planning and thinking about every little detail. It doesn't matter to me. When I have to take treats to my children's classes, I'm not going to spend my entire day dipping pretzels in chocolate and sprinkling them with crushed candy canes. I'll make some cupcakes from a box mix and top them with instant icing and some sprinkles. The children love it. They just want you there in the class. They just want to know that mommy made their friends a treat. It really doesn't matter what you made—they'll love it.

Some moms go overboard, and I think it's unnecessary. A couple of years ago the parents were asked to bring in snacks for field day. Some of the homemade goodies were so elaborate I thought the mommies were competing on *Iron Chef America.* I felt bad for these moms, because the kindergarteners just destroyed the beautiful decorations in about three nanoseconds. It's nice to fuss, but fuss at the right time. Showing off at the school fund-raiser is just crazy. I fuss on the holidays for my family. I fuss when I have company coming over. But most of the other time I take shortcuts and it's just fine.

I want to save my time for what matters. I want to enjoy my house, my guests, and my children. I would rather have a kitchen full of my friends enjoying my food, and I don't care if there are a few crumbs on the floor. My children have their friends over and I let them paint, play, and have fun. I could spend this afternoon straightening out my desk, but I would rather take the kids for a bicycle ride, and then I'll make my kids' favorite meatball heroes for dinner.

Listen, I'm not going to tell you I don't have my own neuroses. I certainly do. I try to cook with, eat, and feed my family an organic diet, but I do let them eat some junk once in a while. I push my children to do great in school, but I back off and let them have fun after school before they do their homework. I should be more of a disciplinarian, but I try not to be so serious with the children because childhood is just not serious. It's the one time in your life when you can totally goof off. All the pressure parents are putting on their children to be accomplished is ridiculous. I choose just one extra activity besides school for the children each semester. I let them run wild in the yard, get dirty, and be kids.

I worry every day that I'm going to find a lump under my arm. I worry every day that my children might be snatched the next time we go to the mall. I worry that one day this entire earth will be completely toxic with no clean food, water, or air left for our grandchildren. Yes, I do worry. But I don't waste my precious time taking all the little things too seriously. So start enjoying your life and stop nit-picking about all the nonsense that doesn't matter.

Laugh It Off

Finally, the weather was nice today. After a long, brutally cold winter being cooped up in this house with the children, spring has finally sprung. Wow, I was excited to just get out of the house. I got dressed with my new low-rise jeans, some flip-flops, and a cute little T-shirt, and I was feeling good. Hey, look at me. I was out the door with Hannah to do some errands and then go to the park. While talking to some other moms I happened to look down to see a little of my belly sticking out between my shirt and pants, which would be a cute look if it weren't for my new old-lady pubic hairs starting to grow and creep their way toward my belly button. Not something I ever had before. I looked down and was horrified as these new hairs were popping out all over the place. I ran home and called my gynecologist. Hormonal changes, he said. "You can expect this, Darla, you're going to be forty."

So I guess this is it. Premenopausal hormonal bullshit. I guess I'm old. I'm not ready for this. I look way too cute to start my changes. I refuse to go through it. I'm going to fight . . . so off I went to get electrolysis. That really hurts, but after a few zaps, my old-lady pubes were gone.

When I got home, I had about an hour and forty five minutes to pull together a birthday dinner for my father, who was expecting homemade lasagna. Connor and Hannah had a playdate scheduled. I was under the gun. As I sautéed the onions and garlic in olive oil while Connor and his friend ran through my house with muddy shoes, and Hannah sat in the kitchen throwing a tantrum because she wanted to go to the park, I just looked around and started to laugh. This was complete chaos. I never know what's going to happen. It's the craziness of it all that I think is great. It makes me laugh. It keeps me surprised. I try not to take anything too seriously. If you let stuff roll off your back, if you can have pride in who you are, if you can stop complaining and start laughing, your entire attitude will change.

So your life is not what you thought it was going to be. So you're not the vice president of the bank. So you're getting hot flashes at night. So your son is not making straight As. So you found out your daughter went to first base on the school bus yesterday. So your husband burned another one of your good pans making eggs for the kids . . . so what? Laugh it off.

You know there's always going to be someone doing better than you and someone doing worse. I try not to think about what anyone else is doing but me. I try not to worry about things that don't matter. Worrying, gossiping, and nit-picking take up way too much time in the day, and ladies, you don't have the time for this stuff. Don't spend even a minute doing something that's going to pull you down. Don't spend time with anyone who is going to pull you down. Look at what's important, don't sweat the small stuff, and laugh.

Tonight I was watching a cute movie, *Under the Tuscan Sun* with Diane Lane. I was in my bed relaxing all by myself; Bill was on a business trip. I put the children to sleep and was finally able to enjoy some time with a chick flick and a glass of wine. Just when I finally got comfortable, I spilled the entire glass of merlot all over me and my chenille comforter. I just had to laugh . . . otherwise, I would have cried.

I was once on the highway stuck in traffic. Hannah was about three months old and screaming her head off. Connor, who was three at the time, suddenly had to do a doody. He was screaming, Hannah got hysterical, and my heart started palpitating. I started to sweat, and I thought I was going to have a nervous breakdown. I tried to pull over, and by the time I did Connor had pooped all over himself and my car. I had no extra clothes for him, and it was beginning to snow. I cried. I wiped up my son as best as I could, and then I sat there in the backseat on the side of the highway as cars passed by and nursed my baby so she would stop screaming.

After that, I made sure I was prepared. I never left the house without my Mommy Emergency Bag. Keep it in your car at all times, along with a blanket and an emergency car kit. You can get that at any auto parts store, or go to www.911kits.com.

Mommy Emergency Bag

1. *Nonperishable snacks that your children really love*
2. *Bottled water and juice*
3. *Regular wipes for face and tushy*
4. *Antibacterial wipes for hands after touching public things like shopping carts*
5. *Tissues*
6. *Liquid Tylenol and dispenser*
7. *Extra set of underpants and clothes for each child*
8. *Plastic baggies for poop and dirty diapers*
9. *Plastic bowl for pooping or peeing in*
10. *Plastic cup for Mommy to pee in (sounds bizarre, but moms, we have all been there. Admit it. I won't give my horrid details, but trust me, it happens.)*
11. *Crayons and coloring books*

Scream!

Go ahead, ask my neighbors. They'll tell you that they hear me screaming my head off all the time. I lose my temper. My children make me crazy. My husband and I argue. I'm not perfect, and neither is life. Life is hard. I think it's much easier to hide out in your bedroom with the sheets pulled over your head than it is to actually deal with the problems. It's easier to pop pills than to face reality. It's easier to drug your kids than to deal with them. This must be why so many women are on antidepressants, and why so many mothers are allowing their children to be diagnosed with behavioral problems and medicated at such young ages. It's because these women cannot cope with reality. It's because we all have a hard time being successful at life. Because we all have this image set for us of what our lives should be, and when it isn't so, we blow up.

I'm a screamer. I have this hot-tempered Italian blood mixed with female bitchiness and hormones, so watch out. Lately, I've been trying not to yell and lose my temper, and instead I stop, breathe, and think . . . a method I learned from the show *Blues Clues*. That little blue dog is right. I've learned to calm myself down when I'm about to lose it. I give myself a time-out. But I must admit that once in a while a good healthy scream makes me feel better.

I understand the dilemma of the at-home mom; it's all harder than you thought it would be. I know. No one warned us about this. From the beginning I've said that being a mom and housewife is the hardest job there is. It's mentally, emotionally, and physically draining. But hiding from our problems will only make matters worse. Bottling up your emotions and not being true to yourself will make you miserable.

While I want you to stop being desperate and start being happy, I've never said and never will say that motherhood is a piece of cake. It can be a nightmare. In fact, the entire process is a nightmare, or at least it was for me. My pregnancy was a fiasco. I had so much gas, bloating, and nausea that I'd lie in front of the toilet and cry every day of my first trimester. With Hannah my uterus started to fall out of my body, and I was bedridden for the last three months. Labor is absolutely animalistic and disgusting as far as I'm concerned. Panting and pushing like an animal in front of your husband—now there's something that could really throw the romance out the window. As I've mentioned, Connor got stuck and the doctors had cut through my ass to get him out. Thank God, we women forget the pain, because Hannah got stuck, too, and the doctor had to sit on my stomach to push her out. A perfect candidate for a C-section, wouldn't you think? And what about what pregnancy and nursing does to your body? My perky B-cup boobs blew up to a size D when I was breast-feeding, only to leave me with two stretched-out breast remnants that won't even fill up an A-cup training bra. I would love to get implants, but since the doctor removed that cyst and I'm trying to eat totally organic, it just doesn't seem right. I would love some perky new boobs, but right now I have other goals. I'm just trying to get Connor to brush his teeth at night. I'm trying to teach my dog not to pee every time someone comes into the house. Every day is exhausting. Hannah doesn't listen to a word I say. Each morning, it takes three hours of her screaming and whining for her to finally pick her outfit out for the day. She's a handful. She was the same way as an infant. She cried all day and all night and nothing made her happy. I was exhausted then, and I remember praying for her to just be quiet. I'm still praying.

It's Okay to Admit That Some Days Really Do Suck

When you're at home with your children day in and day out, when you haven't had a minute alone all day, when the kids are jumping off the walls, when your house is a mess and your husband isn't home, when you have a migraine or a head cold or just want to go for a drive and never come home—it's those days when you think your life really stinks. How can you not feel sorry for yourself?

Some days, I look at my children when they're out of control and I wonder why they're misbehaving, what I'm doing wrong. Some days, my husband and I just get on each other's nerves, and I cannot stand the sight of him. I'm sure he despises me on those days, too. Even the strongest marriages have their bad days. Even the best mother can't stand another second of her daughter tugging at her. Even the most patient mother wants to be left alone sometimes. Some days, I snap, too. I told you earlier that I lost it and gave Connor a smack on his behind just the other day. I felt terrible. I lost control. I don't want to do that again.

As you know, when Connor was small I would not leave him for a minute. I slept with him in my bed, I wore him on my chest all day in a baby carrier, and when he was bigger I moved him onto my back into a backpack. For a year I really never let him go. Looking back now, I can remember having severe back pain. I remember crying because I was exhausted. Still, I was too worried to leave him alone even for a few minutes. I even took him to the bathroom with me. I remember being on the toilet with a horrific stomachache and breast-feeding him at the same time. It's amazing what a mother will do. We all do these things.

I remember one day having a near breakdown. I just wanted to take Connor and throw him across the room. Of course, I didn't. I knew then that I just had to get him off of me. I just had to get some space. I needed to get my body back. I needed to get Darla back. I remember putting him into his crib and he began to cry, and so did I.

I cried because I felt guilty that I was not happy every single minute. I was disappointed in myself for not being perfect. I was living a life that was not real. I was trying so hard to make everything run smoothly that on days when it wasn't, I felt like a failure.

It was like the lyrics of that song: "Mama said there'd be days like this . . ." You know the song—my mother always sang it. She always told me how hard being a mom was and how unappreciated mothers were, but she never warned me about the bad days.

I think it's normal to be angry sometimes, to yell once in a while, to feel like running away sometimes. It's all part of a healthy family. Allowing your children to express their anger, their frustrations, and their emotions is healthy for them. Holding everything in is not healthy for you. But you do need to watch what comes out of your mouth. I've heard parents at the grocery store tell their kids that they're rotten. I've heard husbands tell their wives to f—off. Even on the worst days, when you feel these feelings, remember not to cross the line. Children hate their parents sometimes, and parents hate each other sometimes, but you have to remember that these feelings are temporary and not take it too seriously.

You need to average in the great stuff: the strong bond, the love, the commitment. It makes me so angry that the divorce rate is so high in this country. I would never tell any woman to stay in an abusive marriage, whether it's physical or emotional abuse. I've seen a lot of verbal abuse out there that I would not accept. But I know of a lot of divorces in which one of the spouses simply moved on to greener pastures.

What about the children? It would destroy me to have my children torn between two homes. I would be insanely jealous if my husband remarried and the new stepmom was hanging with my family. Maybe I feel this way because I love my husband—thank God! Maybe couples do fall out of love, and that is reason enough for them to walk away. All I'm saying is that I think a lot of marriages break up too quickly when they should try to stick it out through the rougher times. I always say marriage is like a roller coaster—you go up and down. While I have had some downturns with my husband, the ride has been exciting, and I don't want to get off. When I'm angry with him I try to think of the bigger picture—what life would be like without him, with my kids not having him in their life. I always look down the road. Where do I want to be twenty years from now? I want my family to be together, so maybe it's best to overlook the small stuff.

One of my girlfriends recently confided in me that she thought her husband might be fooling around with another woman. She wanted to confront him and divorce him. I encouraged her to sit down calmly and talk it out. She loved this man, so I asked her if, deep down in her heart, she could live with this. Could she forgive him? Did she want to break up her family? Was she willing to find out why he looked elsewhere in the first place?

It's easy for everyone to judge. It's easy to decide what's good for other people. When it happens to you, you might feel differently. Hey, I always tell my husband that I would kill him if he cheated. But I don't know what I would do. It would be stupid for me to decide now what I might do in the future. Who knows what would happen? I never say never to anything. I know one thing, however—that it's my marriage, and I'll decide what is good for us.

I told my friend to look down the road. Did she want her marriage to stay together or not? It's up to her to decide, not for you or me to point fingers.

So some days really do suck. We all know it. If you think you're going to be happy 100 percent of the time, well, good luck to you. What I've found is that every one of us has our good and bad days, and it's how you handle the bad days that shows your true colors. If you start depending on liquor, drugs, other men, or any act of desperation, you need to stop and get a reality check. Not every day is going to be rosy.

There are days when I, too, think I cannot take another minute. I fight with my husband, too. Sometimes my children are completely out of control. I get lonely, frustrated, and sad.

Today was one of those days. My husband was away on a business trip. I awoke at 4:00 A.M. to my daughter violently projectile vomiting all over my 600-count thread sheets, which I just bought. See what happens when you splurge? Well, her bouts of vomiting kept coming until I finally raced to the emergency room. We sat there all day as doctors poked and prodded her little body. After they gave her some drugs, she fell asleep, and I just sat there and had a breakdown. Who would pick Connor up from the bus stop? Who would go and let our dog out to pee? What if Hannah had appendicitis? Oh no, I should have thrown the sheets into the laundry before I left—and did I shut off the coffee pot? All these images were flashing through my head.

I felt so alone. My husband was on his way back to be with me, but where was he this morning when I had to get Connor off to school, pack a bag, dress Hannah and myself, and get to the emergency room before her appendix ruptured or I had a heart attack? I knew, of course, that there was no way he could have known Hannah was sick, but still, at that moment in the hospital, I resented him. I resented the fact that he's off at work all day in an office, talking to adults, going out to lunch, and being grown-up while I'm always the one carrying the bag.

Like every mom out there, I was the one up night after night when Connor had the croup three times as an infant. I was the one who had to hold Hannah down when she had to get her big toe stitched back on when she was two. I was the one who taught the kids their alphabet, who taught them how to ride their bikes, who does their homework with them, who is responsible for how they look, dress, and act each day. I'm the one who vacuums the kitchen every morning. I'm the one who scrubs the encrusted pee off the toilet every day. I'm the one who chooses the paint for the walls, the fabric for the sofa, the chandelier for the foyer, and the plants for the garden. It is I who prepares the meals, holds it all together—and has the anxiety attack at the hospital.

I was finally able to calm myself down when the doctor diagnosed my daughter. A stomach virus. Ah, I could breathe. . . . Then, as the IV was pulled from Hannah's arm and she howled in pain, my husband finally walked in. He could see that I was pale and ready to snap.

"What can I do to make it better?" he asked.

I didn't have an answer for him. I just shrugged and told him I was tired.

Now, at the end of the day, after the kids have finally fallen asleep, after I have had some herbal tea, I feel relaxed. It's 11:25 P.M., and I have time to sit down and write.

I know what I wanted to tell my husband but didn't, so I'll tell you, my girls out there who I know are living the same mommy roller coaster every single day. I wished I had told him that he just could never get it. He could never really understand how hard it is being at home with the kids. He really does help me when he's home. He bathes the children, plays with them, and straightens up their toys. But he has never been at home day in and day out all alone, holding it all together. I know he thinks his pressures are greater than mine. But I think being responsible for raising two children; keeping a beautiful, clean home; and holding it all together while trying to look good is a lot more pressure.

I've decided that all I really want is some gratitude.

All I want is some respect. I want my husband, every husband—this entire society—to give it up for at-home moms everywhere.

That is what we all want, isn't it? A little respect, a little appreciation, and a little thanks.

So, as I lie here tonight exhausted, writing on my laptop with Hannah sleeping next to me, I think about how hard my day was, about how hard being a mom is, how hard being a wife is, and how hard running a house is. But not for twenty million dollars would I change a bit of it.

I stop and look at my kids. I think about all the children who have cancer or disabilities and I remember how lucky I am. I look at my house and I'm grateful to have such a beautiful home. I consider the fact that my husband has a job and I'm able to put food on the table and clothes on my children, and these are small things that many of us take for granted every day.

Try to Accept the Things You Can't Change

Maybe we all expect too much: the perfect marriage, the perfect house, the perfect kids. Maybe our expectations are too high. I've learned to accept the things I can't change. I spent years agonizing about some family issues that just cannot be resolved. I was devastated when my father-in-law did not come to our wedding. I couldn't believe my husband was disrespected in such a way. But you know what? It was their problem, not mine, so I had to just accept it. One of my girlfriends argues with her husband over the same issue every holiday: his family and how much she dislikes them. She just wants no part of them, and she nags her husband to death about this issue. I have begged her to let it go. Let him be his own person. Let him be with his family if he chooses to. She needs to accept him and the situation for what it is.

As you know, it was really difficult for me to cope with leaving my career. I really didn't have closure until I was able to accept things for what they were—that my destiny at the time was to be with my son. Once I was able to accept it, I was able to start enjoying my baby and my life.

It's sad that so many of us hold on to an image we can't obtain. I have a friend who is devastated because her son is overweight. I have another friend who is miserable because her teenage daughter just told her she thinks she's a lesbian. One of my girlfriends cannot get over the fact that her husband wants a divorce. I'm afraid that she might be suicidal. It's really hard to accept the truth. It's hard to accept what we don't want to happen.

I know. My heart is broken right now because I haven't been able to see my own grandfather in years because of some family squabble. I can't change this. I wish I could. I can't have everything I want in this life. If I could, we would all live peacefully, without poverty and with full health care benefits. I try every day to simply accept things I cannot change, but some days it's really hard to do this.

Life can be very difficult. I'm not perfect. I struggle every day to make it all work. But every day I try to keep a sense of humor. I try to look at the bright side. I try to laugh it off. I try my hardest to be the best mom, the best wife, the best friend, the best woman I can be. I was on the edge. I got my act together, and now it's your turn. Grow up, get real, pull yourself together, and accept the things that you cannot change. Once you start accepting, you'll be happy.

Forgive

I had no intention to write about forgiveness until I just finished the last paragraph. I realize that to be truly happy you have to have forgiveness in your heart. I know many people who are harboring resentment, grudges, and hatred for other people, and all it's doing is eating them up.

I was raised with a huge extended family. Holidays were full of people sharing joy and creating memories. But as I grew up some family members just didn't live up to the image I had created for them. I thought I had this big, fun extended family who stuck together through the good and bad times, but as I became an adult I realized that my family was full of dysfunction, craziness, and a lot of hostility. I learned that I didn't have to try to hold on to this Osmond family image, and I've pretty much accepted that it will never come to fruition. I think we all expect too much from people, especially our family members. I wonder if we would even associate with half of our relatives if we weren't bound my blood and obligation. Maybe my image of what a family should be just isn't realistic. Maybe if we expected less, we would be less surprised.

It took me a long time to accept these things that I cannot change, and I realized I needed to forgive all of the people I knew who were not perfect. My daughter's godmother has completely ignored her since she was born. I harbored so much anger about it that it was driving me crazy. I tried several times to fix that connection and to get this woman to do the right thing by my child. But I cannot change her. I have to forgive her so that I can live in peace. I refuse to hold grudges. I try to understand the other person and forgive their actions. Many women I know are driving themselves batty holding on to grudges, and it's such a waste of time.

One of my friends was angry when she sent a gift to her neighbor that was never acknowledged. Another girlfriend was livid when her neighbor never reciprocated a dinner invitation. My grandfather didn't speak to his sister for forty years over some argument about a chandelier. My mother remembers every dime any relative ever gave her and waits for the day she has to give them a gift just so she can have revenge. This is an Italian thing, I think—an eye for an eye.

I say that you'll never be a happy housewife as long as you harbor resentment, anger, or hatred for another person. You have to just let it go. (I just read that statement to Connor, who says he disagrees . . . he says he would punch the person out.) Well, we moms can't just go around punching out other moms, even if we want to. So, why not put out the olive branch? Or maybe you don't want to make up. At least let go of the torment in your heart. Forgive the other person in your soul. Forget what it was that made you angry to begin with. You can be bigger than this.

I almost forgot about this one—I actually have two friends who broke up their relationship over a banana. Yes, it's true. One mother grabbed the last banana in the fruit bowl and gave it to her daughter. The other mother was so angry that the woman had the nerve to take her last banana that they got into an argument over it. Ladies, how immature can you be?

Don't sweat the small stuff. Accept what you cannot change, and find forgiveness. Be happy, give love and support to your girls, be social, have fun, and stop worrying about what everyone else is doing. Life is just too short for all this nonsense. Ladies, we do act very immaturely sometimes. I think sometimes housewives just get a little bored and like to create drama in their lives. Remember, it's not ladylike to be a bitch. All moms are in the same boat. Let's try to forgive and forget. Let's try to accept and be tolerant. Let's try not to judge each other. And, most importantly, let's all try to support one another.

Remember, You're Strong, You Can Be Great at This

My heart is palpitating. I feel as if I'm going to have a nervous breakdown. For the past three days my oil burner has been broken. The guy comes to fix it, and it shuts off as soon as he pulls out of the driveway. For three days, the kids and I haven't been able to take a hot bath. Good thing it's spring and we don't need heat. I was so upset this morning that I called someone new to come and fix it. I paid four hundred dollars for the honor, and tonight when I was ready to bathe the children the water came out black as oil. I really thought I was going to lose it. Bill, of course, was away on business, and as usual it was up to me to hold it all together. I called the repairman and went berserk. I told him that I was going to have a nervous breakdown.

"Run the water," he said.

"No kidding," I said. "It's been running for an hour and it's still brown."

Why do men think we're idiots? Why do all male physicians, repairmen, even our own husbands think we're either damsels in distress or emotionally crazed hormonal women who cannot think clearly? Why do men ask us such stupid questions?

I just spoke to Bill and was telling him about my horrible day and he said, "Did you call the neighbors to see if their water was running brown, too?" Oh, honey, I didn't think of that. . . . I'm just a dumb blonde.

But the truth is that we sometimes deserve this reputation, don't we? Let's face it, I'm really emotional right now. I did tell the service guy that I was having a nervous breakdown. I just told Bill that I cannot take another minute and that I'm putting the house up for sale tomorrow because the last homeowner put a curse on it and I can't live here with this bad karma. I just told the kids that we're going to move again and to get used to that idea. As I sip my glass of chardonnay—yes, I'm drinking now to calm myself down—I'm in bed with the children, and we all smell of a mixture of dirty bodies, soot, and oil.

I have to just get a grip and try to laugh this off. I screamed earlier at Connor as I walked into the kitchen and saw him gulping down a big glass of dirty, parasite-ridden water. I lost it and scared the crap out of him. I did feel better after screaming for a while. Sometimes screaming is just the therapy you need when you're upset. I felt better.

Of course, my second glass of the old spirits is making me a bit relaxed, too. Now, as I lie here, I guess I should count my blessings. I should meditate. I should follow my own advice and stop whining and complaining. I know what I'm supposed to do, and I guess that's what I have to do in order to get past this. It really is ridiculous in the grand scheme of things. To have a night of brown water isn't really that big a deal, is it? Tomorrow is another day, as Scarlett O'Hara said.

So even though my husband isn't here, I'm home alone again with the kids, and something huge has happened, I'm not going to let it get me. I'm not going to become a desperate housewife. I am strong, I am woman.

But it's always something, right? You know what I'm talking about. There's always some fiasco, some crisis, something to deal with, and we rarely get a break. It's hard to hold it all together. Being a mom is the hardest job there is. But you're strong, and you can and will be great at it.

When you think you're going to lose it, talking to other women is great therapy. You can find moms blogging and chatting on the Internet on any number of sites:

- www.dot-moms.com. There are hundreds of mommy blog sites listed there.
- www.ivillage.com. A network of women discussing issues that affect women.

- And, of course, you could always visit me at www.darlashine.com.
- If you seriously feel blue and are worried you might have postpartum depression, please visit www.mommy-muse.com.
- If you have older children and feel depressed, try www.depression.com.
- If you feel as if you have low self-esteem, please visit www.selfesteem 4women.com.

Don't Wish for Someone Else's Problems

Why the grass isn't always greener

Remember, you only have one shot at this

Savor every moment

So you think you have it bad. You think your problems are big.

I hope it isn't so. I wish for you to have health, happiness, and love. As I write this particular step, I'm in my kitchen, as usual, and the news just broke that the pope has passed away. Pope John Paul II has made his way to heaven. God bless his soul. God bless all of ours. It doesn't matter if you're Catholic or Protestant, Republican or Democrat, the common bond that we women share is stronger than any political party or organized religion. We're mothers. We all want the same thing for our families. We want health, joy, love, and to live safely in peace together while we're on earth.

I was originally going to talk about a different perspective in this step, but the news of this pope's passing, and something that he said, has made me think that his message is way bigger than the one I wanted to write about. My angle was going to be that you should never think that your problems are so big that you wish for someone else's, because you thought their problems were fewer. Thinking about the pope and all he stood for has made me turn my thinking on this around a bit. Perhaps we should consider other people's problems more than our own. Isn't that the better way? Maybe if we did consider other women, other mothers, other children, other families a little more, we could all help ease one another's sorrows.

Really, do we want our babies to have full stomachs while our neighbors' babies cry in hunger? Do we want our children to be safe in gated communities while our sisters' children dodge bullets on their way to school? Do we want only our babies to have a future full of hope, while our sisters' babies have none?

I wish I had more courage to actually do more. My friends Dina and Claire flew to China to adopt infant girls. My friend Dana flew to Russia to bring home two children who were living in orphanages and would have been let out onto the streets when they were only nine years old to fend for themselves. I wonder what's holding me back from doing more to help save a child. I know it's just pure laziness and lack of commitment. I feel so guilty now. I just heard that the pope accused Westerners of being too materialistic and losing our capacity for compassion. I think he was right. Look around you. Look at what we have in this country. Imagine how wonderful it would be if none of our children went hungry. Imagine what a great society we would have if all of our children had a home, decent clothes, health care, and hope.

How embarrassing it is for all of us that we're so consumed with getting breast implants, Botox, the latest fashions, and the designer handbag, and how disgraceful it is for any of us to complain or say that we're desperate. Think about the true desperation around the world—and right here in our own country. What are you going to do to help? What am I going to do? We have to come together to do something.

I know I'm getting really deep—frankly, deeper than I expected to go. You know, when you write, the process just starts to take over and the words flow onto the page, and all I can say is that we—the women, the mothers, the warriors—have to do more.

I'm so ashamed. I went shopping yesterday and spent money on a lot of stuff I didn't need. Why didn't I write a check to a charity instead? I want my water to be clean, but I've never done a damned thing to fight for clean water. I want all children in the world to be fed, but did I ever volunteer or do anything to help bring food to the world?

Like many of us, I'm full of it. I say I want all these things, but I've really done nothing at all. I've been consumed with raising my own children, trying to have a good marriage, and worrying about all my problems, complaining when everything isn't perfect, and wishing for all the wrong things. I daydream about my son going to MIT when other mothers just hope that their sons will survive cancer. I get upset that my daughter doesn't want to take acting lessons, while other mothers are searching for their missing daughters. I complain that my husband works too much, when other women pray for their husbands to find work.

If I hope to do anything with this book, it's to inspire mothers out there to do more in this life—this one shot that we have to get it all done. We all spend too much time worrying about our own problems. We all waste too much time complaining, whining, gossiping, and nagging about nonsense. I hope we can stop. Really, sit back and take a look at your life. How lucky are you that you can read this book in peace in your own home without a soldier with a gun staring you down. Think about how lucky you are that tomorrow morning you get to wake up again. Think about how your children are tucked safe and sound in their warm beds tonight. Think about your life so far and all the wonderful memories you have. Think about what you want to do with the rest of it. Think about the big picture, down the road, how you want to look back on yourself and your contribution to this world.

You could take pride in the fact that you're a mother, and that is the most important contribution to this world that you could make. You could be confident in the choices that you've made to be at home to care for your family. You could look forward to spending a lifetime with the man that you love. You're lucky because you have so much to look forward to.

So I have to ask you to please, when you think you're desperate, when you think that you cannot handle being at home with the kids, when you think your life stinks, think again.

We're very lucky. In this book I've asked you to make your house a beautiful home for your family. I've asked you to stop annoying your husband and start turning up the heat in the bedroom. I've encouraged you to go out and buy some new clothes and get a new hairdo. I've said you need to make time for yourself and to never ever give up your dreams. But I have one more thing to ask of you: that you do not forget your sisters' problems. Please help other mothers who desperately need help. Let's vow to save the act of desperation for those in true need. Let's use our time to come together and do something that would really make an impact. Let's help lift other mothers up. Let's start up where the feminist movement left off. Let's not just look the other way. Can't we fight for this? Maybe if we all have this bigger goal, then we won't have so much time left over to wallow in sorrow. What do you think?

Why the Grass Isn't Always Greener

We always tend to think the grass is greener in our neighbors' yards. But I'm looking outside right now, and the grass is looking pretty green. I think a lot of us waste so much time in envy about what our neighbors and friends have, about how wonderful their lives must be. But the truth is that every family has its problems. Every family has something going on. No family is perfect.

The other day I was on a ferry with Bill and the children. We were coming home from Connecticut over the Long Island Sound. We were up there looking for houses, because I'm crazy and always looking to move. I was sitting next to a woman who had a little girl, and we began chatting as her daughter and Hannah began to play together. I have a knack for starting conversations with women and grilling them about their lives. She started to tell me about all the horrible things going on in her life and her community. One child down the block recently died of some rare disease, another child a few blocks over was just killed in a car crash, a teenager in the neighborhood had cancer, another teenager killed his father with a samurai sword, and she was getting freaked out about it all and was thinking of packing up her family and moving away from all the misery. She also told me that her mom died recently of pancreatic cancer, and that she herself was divorced and trying to raise seven children. She was worried about how she was going to afford to pay rent, because Long Island was just so expensive.

I looked at her, this pretty girl, with so much on her shoulders. She looked about the same age as me, and she had so much more to deal with. Here I was looking for a new house, a bigger house. Why? Because I had too much time on my hands, because I had some extra money to buy a bigger home, with my husband who, thank God, has a great job, and two children who, thank God, we can afford. Here I was acting like a spoiled brat, trying to trade up to a better house, and here was this girl with all these problems just trying to stay afloat.

I think there are messages out there for us every day. I think everything happens for a reason. If we open our eyes and our ears, we can learn important lessons about life at any moment. When I got home yesterday afternoon, I looked at Bill and said, "You know, I'm really a jerk. Look at our house—it really is beautiful. We really have everything. Most important, we have our health. Our children are healthy. I know I met that woman on the ferry to snap me back into reality."

When I came into the house, I took a few minutes to listen to my own advice. I sat back and started to count my blessings. I apologized to myself and to God for taking all that I have for granted.

Remember, You Have Only One Shot at This

The one big thing that I have to tell myself over and over every single day is that I have only one shot at this, and I cannot screw it up. I think we all forget how short our lives are. We forget that before we know it our children will be gone, off in the world with their own lives. We forget how precious our time with our young families really is. That we can choose to be happy or miserable. That we can choose to make our marriages strong or weak. That we can choose to be better than we are.

We have all been given this chance at life for a purpose. If you can have faith in that, then I believe you'll be happier. If you can understand that we all are a smaller part of something great, we can all come together and really accomplish something.

We all have only one shot at this life.

Savor Every Moment

Smell your babies. Go play with your son. Make a cake with your daughter. Cuddle with your husband. Enjoy your time with your family. Life is short, so please savor every moment.

I cannot wait until tomorrow. Bill is home from work, I'm going to make a big batch of fluffy banana pancakes in the morning, we'll go to church, and we'll spend the day together as a family. No plans, just hanging around the house together playing some games, maybe watch a movie together, who knows? The important thing is that we will be together, that we're a family, and that I'm lucky enough to know how lucky I am.

DARLA'S FAVORITE RESOURCES

My Favorite Information Source

I love AOL, and I think it's great for moms. I love turning my computer on in the morning, and right there I can get the weather, my daily recipes, craft ideas, the latest news, an online calendar, and search engines.

For Daily News

Read the newspaper every day. I subscribe online because I can't bother to walk down to the end of my driveway every morning, especially in the winter. My newspapers are *USA Today* and the *New York Times*—and, of course, for the real news, *Star* magazine—or read your favorite local newspaper.

Must-Read Monthly Magazines

Martha Stewart Living
O, the Oprah Magazine
Ladies' Home Journal
Good Housekeeping
Redbook
More (if you're over thirty-five)

Parenting
Newsweek

Save a lot of money by subscribing—and if you subscribe long-term, up to three years, you save an enormous amount. Keep close track of when you subscribe, what you pay, and when it expires so that you don't pay twice or interrupt delivery.

Looking for a New House?

www.realtor.com

Advice for Women

www.dot-moms.com
www.mommyblog.com
www.ivillage.com.
www.mommy-muse/com

There's a great book you should buy: *You Can Do It* by Lauren Catuzzi Grandcolas (San Francisco: Chronicle, 2005), who sadly died on September 11, 2001, on United Airlines flight 93. This is a wonderful handbook filled with skills you should master, from changing a tire to sewing a button.

Cooking

www.mrbreakfast.com. There are dozens of great ideas for breakfast here.
www.foodnetwork.com. Some of my favorite chefs—Bobby Flay, Tyler Florence, Ina Garten (the Barefoot Contessa), Paula Dean, and, of course, Rachael Ray—all have wonderful recipes on this site. Also tune in to the network during the day to see them in action and get more ideas.
www.marthastewart.com. I always turn to Martha when I'm having company.
www.epicurious.com
www.meals.com
www.cookinglight.com. The name says it all—great recipes full of flavor with few calories.

www.lhj.com (Ladies Home Journal). I like their seasonal ideas.

www.southernliving.com. This is a great site when you're throwing a party or having a holiday get-together. I love their appetizer ideas.

www.cocktail.com. For when you want to whip up something great—an apple martini, a peach margarita, a cosmopolitan, a mojito, or any other drink you have no idea how to make.

www.ehow.com. Go here to learn how to do anything from how to make a hard-boiled egg, how to fry an egg, how to make shrimp cocktail, how to pick out the right shrimp, the freshest vegetables, and any other questions you could have.

www.williams-sonoma.com

www.surlatable.com

Healthy Food Sources

www.mannaharvest.net

www.taquitos.net

www.villageorganics.com

www.wellnessgrocer.com

Exercise

www.jorgecruise.com

The Ultimate New York Body Plan by David Kirsch (New York: McGraw-Hill, 2004)
Workout tapes by Kathy Smith DETAILS TK

Health

www.drgreene.com

www.kidshealth.org

www.keepkidshealthy.com

www.wrongdiagnosis.com

www.shirleyswellnesscafe.com

www.mercola.com

www.vh.org (Virtual Hospital)

Cleaning

www.homemadesimple.com

www.heloise.com

www.queenofclean.com

www.organizetips.com

www.organizedhome.com

www.getorganizednow.com

Decorating

www.getdecorating.com

www.bhg.com (Better Homes and Gardens)

www.hgtv.com

Spirituality

In Sweet Company: Conversations with Extraordinary Women About Living a Spiritual Life by Margaret Wolff (San Diego: Margaret Wolff Unlimited, 2004)

www.insweetcompany.com

Imagine: What America Could Be in the 21st Century by Marianne Williamson (Emmaus, PA: Daybreak, 2000)

Everyday Grace: Having Hope, Finding Forgiveness, and Making Miracles by Marianne Williamson (New York: Riverhead Books, 2002)

www.marianne.com

www.susankramer.com

www.chickensoup.com

A FEW FINAL THOUGHTS

You Can Be a Good Friend

Close friendships are crucial for the housewife. If it weren't for my circle of girls when my children were young, I would have probably spiraled into a deep depression. Those long hours of sitting on the floor building blocks are much easier when another mom and baby are there for company. We moms need some adult stimulation during the day. We need to share. We need other women.

So open yourself up for a real relationship with other mothers. Don't be a gossip. Don't talk about other women. And when you meet women like this—the nasty girls— just stay away.

You Can Be a Great Mom

As you know, being a mom is the most important thing you'll ever do. So, while it's a job that once you start you'll do for the rest of your life, there really is no time for slacking off. You may take a rest from time to time, but you'll always have to be on your toes. You can be a great mom if you don't get crazy in the process.

You Can Be an Amazing Lover

I say this because I believe sex is the absolute number one thing in a marriage. Forget all that communication stuff—call your girlfriends to talk. I'm talking about sex. You have to have intimacy on a regular basis to stay close with your spouse. If you're not getting the action you want, and if you're not giving the action he wants, you'll both be miserable and your marriage won't be strong. You might stay together, but in isolation. Now that is desperation.

You Can Keep a Happy Marriage

Besides having hot, steamy sex with your hubby, there's something a lot of women do that leads to their men straying. They don't know when to shut their mouths. Men just cannot handle hearing that they're jerks, or stupid, or any other insult you want to throw their way when they forget to take the garbage out. Just zip it.

You Can Get in Shape

You really must do this not only for your husband, but for yourself and your children. You need to get yourself on a diet, out of the house and exercising, and into shape. If your husband is a blob on the couch, you have to get him in shape too. Yes, it's your responsibility. Get moving. If you look good and feel good, it will make you happier.

You Can Do It

I'm living proof that you can have a beautiful, clean house; good kids who are smart and healthy; a satisfying sex life; and a happy marriage without losing your marbles. It can be done. If you have a schedule and you take time each day for yourself, you can make it work. My husband leaves at 5:00 in the morning and comes home at 9:00 in the evening. I see many women who have husbands who come home at 6:00 for dinner, and they complain that they cannot do it all. Well, I do it all, and without the help of my husband, so get your act together. Play with your kids. Clean your house. Cook a homemade meal.

You Should Do It

Let's embrace our wifehood, our motherhood, our womanhood. Let's be the generation who finally says yes, we have the freedom to explore our sexuality; yes, we have the education and the opportunities; yes, we have almost equal power in the workforce; yes, we have most of the spending power; yes, we can be all these things—but we choose to do what our hearts tell us.

We choose to go back home. We choose to be with our children. We choose to be housewives. We choose to be homemakers. We choose to let our husbands be the breadwinners. We choose to not let all that we have fought for as women to now be portrayed as stupid, strung out, like desperate housewives. We're smarter than that.

Well, I cannot believe it, but here I am. Let's see—it's 12:12 A.M. on May 11, and I just finished writing this book. I feel as if I'm at the end, yet I don't want to stop! I feel as if I've said what I need to say, and I hope I've helped at least one woman find happiness— or at least have a few laughs. I love you all.

Please write to me at www.darlashine.com.

ACKNOWLEDGMENTS

I can't believe I'm actually writing an acknowledgments page. This means I'm at the end of the process, and soon this book will be printed and on the store shelves. This has been a dream come true for me. I'm so lucky, and I know it. I'm going to enjoy every second of it.

I wish I could meet every one of you. Any mom who has taken the time out of her hectic schedule to sit down and read what I have to say, I thank you. I wish you all the very best.

It's so hard to write this part of the book. There are so many amazing people in my life who helped make this dream a reality.

To Judith Regan, my publisher. Thank you for believing in me. You were great to work with. You supported my ideas, and you're a remarkable, brilliant woman and mother. To Cassie Jones, my editor. I think you're great. You remained calm through all my madness. I hope you're inspired to go home for awhile and have a baby.

To all the people at ReganBooks. You were all excited about this project from the very start, and each of you has been an enormous asset. I couldn't have done this without you. Thank you so much.

To Melanie Dunea. I'm honored that you were my photographer. You captured it all. I think you're an amazing artist.

• •

To all my friends. I'm so fortunate to have you in my life. You bring me so much joy.

To my godmother, Angela. You've inspired me more than you know.

To my sister, Cheryl, and my nephew, Ryan. Thank you for being part of my life.

To my parents, Camille and Artie. No matter what crazy scheme I've come up with, you were both there to back me up. You gave me confidence. You gave me life. Thanks are not enough.

To my grandmother, Josie. Your spirit lives on through me. You're my guardian angel.

To my husband, Bill. From the first day we met you were always my biggest fan. You have supported me and given me the freedom to be at home with my children. I am grateful.

To Connor and Hannah. Every day I look at you and I know I'm blessed. You both are the light of my life.

To God! Thank you for answering my prayers.